British-American Genealogical Research
Monograph Number 9, Part 1 and Part 2,
and Monograph Number 10

BRITISH AND GERMAN DESERTERS, DISCHARGEES, AND PRISONERS OF WAR WHO MAY HAVE REMAINED IN CANADA AND THE UNITED STATES, 1774–1783: PART 1 AND PART 2

[and]

DESERTERS AND DISBANDED SOLDIERS FROM BRITISH, GERMAN, AND LOYALIST MILITARY UNITS IN THE SOUTH, 1782

Clifford Neal Smith

CLEARFIELD

*British and German Deserters, Dischargees, and
Prisoners of War Who May Have Remained in
Canada and the United States, 1774–1783: Part 1*
Copyright © 1988 by Clifford Neal Smith
All Rights Reserved.
Originally published
McNeal, Arizona, 1988

*British and German Deserters, Dischargees, and
Prisoners of War Who May Have Remained in
Canada and the United States, 1774–1783: Part 2*
Copyright © 1989 by Clifford Neal Smith
All Rights Reserved.
Originally published
McNeal, Arizona, 1989

*Deserters and Disbanded Soldiers from British,
German, and Loyalist Military Units in the South, 1782*
Copyright © 1991 by Clifford Neal Smith
All Rights Reserved.
Originally published
McNeal, Arizona, 1991

Reprinted, 3 Parts in 1, for
Clearfield Company, Inc. by
Genealogical Publishing Co., Inc.
Baltimore, Maryland
2004

International Standard Book Number: 0-8063-5257-4

Made in the United States of America

British-American Genealogical Research
Monograph Number 9, Part 1

BRITISH AND GERMAN DESERTERS, DIS-
CHARGEES, AND PRISONERS OF WAR WHO
MAY HAVE REMAINED IN CANADA AND THE
UNITED STATES, 1774-1783: PART I

Clifford Neal Smith

First printing, April 1988   UZ
Reprint, May 1989   qz
Reprint, January 1990   qz
Reprint, March 1992   u
Reprint, November 1993   u
Reprint, January 1996   u

INTRODUCTION

The identification of enemy soldiers who remained in the American States (and Canada) after the Revolution is of obvious usefulness to the genealogical researcher. In a series of studies of the mercenaries brought over by the British government as members of German military units, thousands of deserters have been identified and their places of origin in the Old Country established.[1] Similar studies of soldiers (both British and German) brought over in British military units are still only partial. Discovering the places of origin of these men may be more difficult than it has been for the German mercenaries and will entail search of pay and personnel records in the Public Record Office, London.

Based upon the experience gained from study of the muster rolls of German mercenaries and the subsequent careers of some of those who remained in America after the Revolution, it can be said that two facts are useful in predicting where deserters or prisoners--presumably the British as well as the German ones--are likely to have settled in America: (a) time and place of desertion or captivity; (b) circumstances under which desertion became possible or capture was made. Contrary to expectations, deserters seem seldom to have gone very far from the point of desertion; usually, they were able to find safe haven on the American side of the lines within 20-100 miles of their former unit's place of cantonment. Thus, a deserter from a German or British military unit stationed in Boston is almost certain to have remained in New England; a prisoner of war at the battle of Brandywine will be most likely to have lived thereafter to the south and west of that battleground in southeastern Pennsylvania.

Groups of soldiers often deserted together. Researchers finding a deserter of interest in this monograph should look through the regimental list in which found to determine whether other soldiers of his regiment deserted at the same time. If so, one is likely to find them in later American civil records (censuses, land records, etc.) living near each other, thus making identification more positive.

The names presented hereinafter have been taken from the huge collection of muster rolls in the British Record Office, archival group War Office 12, for the period beginning about 1774 (if the military unit was already stationed in America) to 1783 (when the British units were withdrawn from American soil at the end of the Revolution).

---

1. Deserters from Hessen and Waldeck will be found in <u>Hessische Truppen in amerikanischen Unabhaengigkeitskreig (Hetrina). Veroeffentlichungen der Archivschule Marburg.</u> 5 volumes (Marburg: The Archives, 1976-). Deserters from the remaining troop units sent to America by German principalities (Braunschweig, Ansbach and Bayreuth, Hessen-Hanau, and Anhalt-Zerbst) will be found among the monographs in the German-American Genealogical Research Series (McNeal, AZ: Westland Publications, 1976-). All were compiled by Clifford Neal Smith, excepting that for Anhalt-Zerbst which was compiled by Virginia DeMarce.

I

DESERTERS, DISCHARGEES, AND PRISONERS OF WAR FROM THE FOURTH REGIMENT OF FOOT (KING'S OWN)[1]

The muster rolls for the Fourth Regiment of Foot are to be found in War Office 12, volume 2194. The following list of names has been gleaned from nine muster rolls therein, as follows:

Muster Roll[2]	Where Prepared	Date
A	Boston camp	29 Jun 1774
B	Boston camp	15 Jan 1775
C	Boston camp	08 Sep 1775
D	Boston camp	23 Jan 1776
E	Staten Island	10 Jul 1776
F	New York	30 Dec 1776
G	Philadelphia	23 Feb 1778
H	Philadelphia	06 Feb 1778
I	NY Island	23 Jul 1778
J	NY Island	22 Jul 1778

The muster rolls for 1777 and 1779 are missing and those for 1780 are from St. John's, Antigua, British West Indies.

A history of the King's Own Regiment was not available in the British Museum;[3] but the following chronolgy of engagements in which the Regiment was active has been reconstructed from Fortescue's History of the British Army.[4]

---

00 000 1774   From the muster rolls themselves it is obvious that the Fourth Regiment was already stationed at Boston before the outbreak of the Revolution.

19 Apr 1775   At the battle of Concord and Lexington all companies of the Regiment were engaged, along with other British units. Casualties were heavy.

17 Jun 1775   The flank company only participated in the battle of Bunker Hill. Again, British losses were severe.

03 Jul 1776   After being transported to Staten Island, the Regiment became part of the British First Brigade with its headquarters at Brooklyn.

15 Nov 1776   The Regiment participated in the engagement at Haarlem Creek and the capture of Fort Washington.

25 Apr 1777   A party from the Fourth Regiment (with men from other units) made a raid from New York to Danbury, Connecticut. The enterprise was intercepted on its return march and compelled to fight every yard of its retreat with a loss of 360 men killed or wounded out of a total party of 2,000 (18%).

The Regiment is not further mentioned in Fortescue's very detailed work, until its removal to the West Indies in 1780, so that it be assumed that it spent the years 1778 and 1779 without great activity.

On the list which follows the citations in parentheses are to the nine muster rolls, followed by a page number indicating the place where the muster-roll entries will be found in W.O. 12, volume 2194.

ALEXANDER, John, deserted 7 Feb 1778 (G:225)

ANDERSON, William, drummer, prisoner/rebels (E:195)

ANDREW(S), Alexander, sergeant, prisoner/rebels (G:211; G:223)

ANDREWS, Peter, sergeant, prisoner/rebels (E:197)

BAILESS, William, discharged 8 Jul 1774 (B:161)

BECTMAN, John,[5] discharged (G:218)

BENNICK, Christopher,[6] prisoner/rebels (G:223)

BENTLEY, Peter, prisoner (C:170)

BINDLER? Antony,[6] prisoner/rebels (G:213)

BONEY, Thomas, discharged 24 Dec 1775 (D:186)

BRINDLEY, James, discharged 24 Apr 1774 (A:151)

BROADERICK, Daniel, deserted 5 Apr 1778 (I:234)

BROADHEAD, Samuel, prisoner/rebels (E:199; G:229; I:237)

BROWNMULLIER (BROWNMILLER), Ludwick,[7] prisoner/rebels (G:210; G:220; I:230)

BRUMBY, James, discharged 8 Jul 1777 (G:212)

BRUMBY, Thomas, discharged 8 Jul 1777 (G:225)

BURN, Richard, corporal, prisoner/rebels (G:227)

BURROW(S), John, corporal, prisoner/rebels (E:194; F:206)

BURTON, Duke (or Marmaduke), sergeant, prisoner/rebels (E:193; F:204; G:212; G:225; I:233)

CHESTERFIELD, William, prisoner (B:165)

COLEMAN, John, discharged 23 Feb 1777 (G:218)

COLTON (or Cotton), Henry, deserted 24 Dec 1777 (G:226)

COOK, Peter,[6] deserted 25 Dec 1775 (E:196)

CRAWFORD, Robert, discharged 24 Apr 1778 (I:237)

DEVELYN, Arthur, prisoner/rebels (G:210; G:220)

DOOZLEY, Samuel,[6] discharged 24 Apr 1778 (I:232)

DOYAL, James, prisoner (F:205)

DUNN, Andrew, discharged 23 Aug 1776 (F:206)

EAMES, Robert, discharged 23 Feb 1777 (G:215)

EGGLETON, Thomas, prisoner/rebels (G:218; G:229; I:237)

FAITHFULL, William, deserter 6 Dec 1777 (H:228)

FALL, Francis, prisoner/rebels (E:197; G:211; G:223; J:239)

FAMDEN?, John, deserted 24 Sep 1777 (G:225)

FENIMORE, Humphrey?, discharged 24 Apr 1774 (A:152)

FISHBACK, Dennis,[8] deserted 11 Jun 1777 & 4 Oct 1777 (G:217; G:226)

FLEMMING, Andrew, sergeant, discharged 24 Apr 1778 (I:237)

FRAZER, James, prisoner/rebels (G:218; G:224; I:234)

GARDINER, John, deserted 23 Sep 1774 (B:164)

GOOD, Arthur, discharged 4 Feb 1774 (A:152)

GUYE, Thomas, deserted 23 Dec 1774 (B:164)

HAMILTON, James, discharged 24 Dec 1775 (D:186)

HAMILTON, William, deserted 20 Jun 1778 (I:238)

HARNOTT, John, prisoner/rebels (I:234)

HATFIELD, John, sergeant, discharged 10 Mar 1777 (G:217)

HAZLEHURST, John, deserted 6 Mar 1778 (I:238)

HEATHERLY, Thomas, deserted 25 Jun 1774 (B:167)

HENLY, James, prisoner (G:223)

HERBERT, William, discharged 24 Apr 1778 (I:234)

HILL, John, discharged 24 Apr 1774 (A:158)

HOBBINGS, Jacob, discharged 24 Dec 1775 (D:186)

HOLDEN, John, prisoner/rebels (C:175; D:187; E:194; F:206)

HOLLAND, John, prisoner/rebels (G:213; G:221; I:231)

HUGHS, Andrew, deserted 9 Jun 1777 (G:215)

JAMISON (JEMMISON), Joseph, prisoner/rebels (E:195; F:202; I:235)

JARMAN, Daniel, discharged 23 Feb 1777 (G:211)

JONES, Robert, discharged 10 Nov 1775 (D:182)

JONES, Robert, discharged 23 Feb 1777? (G:211)

KENNADY, Nathaniel, discharged 24 Aug 1777 (G:212; G:225)

KAVENAUGH, Thomas, deserted 9 Nov 1777 (H:228)

KEY, John, deserted 2 Sep 1774 (B:160)

LANGFORD, Thomas, discharged 24 Dec 1775 (D:187)

LAWRENCE (LORANCE), William, prisoner/rebels (F:204; G:212; G:225; I:233)

LING, George, discharged 11 Feb 1774 (A:153)

LOWE, Samuel, discharged 24 Dec 1775 (E:188)

LUMPIE, Anthony, deserted 22 Nov 1775 (G:210)

LYTCH, John Peter, deserted 22 Jun 1778 (J:239)

MABBERLY, Joseph, prisoner (I:232)

McDONALD, Angus, prisoner/rebels (G:217; G:226; I:232)

McGEE, James, discharged 22 Apr 1777 (G:214)

McHARRY, James, prisoner/rebels (F:204; G:212; G:225; I:233)

McKELLER, Dougal, corporal, prisoner/rebels (E:197; F:207; G:211; G:223)

McKINZIE, Valentine, prisoner/rebels (E:190; F:200; G:210; G:220; I:230)

McVEAGH, Edward, prisoner/rebels (G:213; G:221; I:231)

MANEY, William, prisoner/rebels (G:212; G:225; I:233)

MARLOW, Samuel, deserted 12 Apr 1778 (I:232)

MARSH, James, prisoner/rebels (G:216; H:228)

MATTHEWS, James, deserted 18 Apr 1778 (I:237)

MIDDLEWOOD, Robert, prisoner/rebels (G:216; H:228)

MORREANCE? (MORSANCE?), Conrade,[9] prisoner/rebels (G:215; G:227; I:236)

MOSS, Joseph, discharged 24 Aug 1775 (D:188)

MULLEN, Brian, deserted 8 Jul 1774 (B:168)

NEALING, James, prisoner (E:195)

OAKES, Thomas, discharged 25 Jun 1774 (B:167)

ORD, George, sergeant, discharged 24 Apr 1778 (I:233)

PARVIS, Ben, discharged (F:204)

PEET, John, discharged 24 Apr 1774 (A:156)

QUIN, Thomas, deserted 22 Sep 1777 or 22 Dec 1777 (G:213; G:221)

REED, William, prisoner (B:169)

RIELY, Patrick, prisoner (E:195)

RIVETT, James, discharged 24 Apr 1774 (A:150)

SEBERT, Henry,[6] deserted 27 Jun 1774 (A:154)

SEEDS, James, deserted 2 Sep 1777 (H:228)

SHIBLIE, John,[6] deserted 11 Jun 1778 (I:236)

SHIPLEY, John, discharged 24 Dec 1775 (D:183)

SHLYGEN, Peter,[10] deserted 6 Feb 1777 (G:212)

SILLS, William, discharged 24 Apr 1778 (I:236)

SILVIE, Benjamin, discharged 23 Feb 1776 (G:211)

SMITH, Francis, deserted, 22 Jun 1778 (I:233)

SMITH, Nathan, deserted 10 Nov 1775 (D:181)

SMITH, Samuel, prisoner/rebels (G:215; G:227; I:236)

SPEAKER, John, deserted 22 Jun 1778 (I:237)

SPENDLER, Anthony,[6] prisoner/rebels (G:221; I:231)

STAYDON, William, discharged 23 Jan 1774 (A:152)

STOLLARD, Robert, discharged 23 Feb 1777 (G:215)

STRACHAN, John, prisoner/rebels (E:199; G:218; G:229; I:237)

STROUD, John, discharged 23 Feb 1776 (G:211)

SWARTS, Leonard,[11] prisoner/rebels (G:211; G:223; I:239)

TAFT, Thomas, prisoner/rebels (E:198; G:213; G:221)

TAMFREY, William, prisoner/rebels (G:210; I:230)

THIFRIES?, Frederick, deserted 18 Jun 1778 (I:233)

THOMSON (or THOMPSON), John, deserted 24 Dec 1777 (G:215; G:227)

TIMINSON (or TOMINSON), Joseph, prisoner/rebels (G:219; G:224)

TRACEY, James, deserted 18 Jun 1778 (I:231)

VAN HAUSEN, John,[6] corporal (or sergeant), deserted 24 Oct 1777 (G:212; G:225)

VOWELLS, John, discharged 24 Apr 1778 (I:231)

WALLNE?, John, discharged 24 Apr 1774 (A:155)

WARRAN, William, prisoner/rebels (G:212; G:225; I:233)

WATERS William, deserted (F:201)

WATSON, James, discharged 23 Feb 1777 (G:212)

WEST, Richard, discharged 24 Apr 1774 (A:156)

WHITWHAM, William, deserted 23 Sep 1774 (B:163)

WRANGHAM, George, prisoner/rebels (I:234)

---

1. These names were first published in the National Genealogical Society Quarterly, volume 66, number 3 (September 1978), pp. 183-187.

2. The writer's designation for purposes of citation only.

3. There was a card reference, however, to a 152-page monograph, entitled <u>Historical Records, Etc. [of the] Fourth, or King's Own Regiment of Foot, 1680-1839</u>, compiled by R. Cannon in 1839. This work was not immediately available in the British Museum. Further, there is a regimental collection in the Lancaster Museum, Old Town Hall, Market Square, Lancaster, Lancs., which has not been consulted by this writer.

4. John William Fortescue, <u>History of the British Army</u> (London: Macmillan & Co., 1902). This thirteen-volume work is an exhaustive treatment of the subject.

5. Probably a German; if so, the surname would be Bechtmann.

6. Possibly a German.

7. Certainly a German; the name should be Ludwig Braunmueller or Braunmiller.

8. Certainly a German; the name should be Toennies Fischbach; the name Toennies is a Rhenish variation of Anthony.

9. Certainly a German; probably the name should be Conrad Mohranz, or a variation thereof.

10. Certainly a German; the name should be Peter Schleichen.

11. Certainly a German; the name should be Leonhard Schwartz or Schwarz.

II

DESERTERS, DISCHARGEES, AND PRISONERS OF WAR FROM THE FIFTH REGIMENT OF FOOT (NORTHUMBERLAND FUSILIERS)

The British Fifth Regiment of Foot, also called the Northumberland Fusiliers, was an active and probably well-trained unit which had been active in suppressing the disturbances in Ireland beginning in 1771. The Regiment remained in Ireland "until the unfortunate misunderstanding between Great Britain and her North American Colonies assumed an aspect so formidable, that it was deemed necessary to send additional forces to that country."[1]

The movements of the Fifth Regiment on the North American continent during the American Revolution were as follows:

- 7 May 1774, embarked at Monkstown, near Cork, Ireland, for America.

- Beginning of July 1774, landed at Boston, Massachusetts, recently "the scene of violence and outrage, particularly of the destruction of an immense consignment of Tea by the provincials."[2] The Regiment was encamped near the town for some time, until fortifications could be constructed.

- 18 Apr 1775, companies of the Fifth Regiment embarked in boats and proceeded up the Charles River, landed on the marshes of Cambridge, and entered the village of Lexington. After a skirmish at this place, the troops continued their march to Concord. Here, the British were forced to retire, returning exhausted to Charlestown from a march of about 35 miles on a hot day.

- 17 Jun 1775, a body of troops, of which the Fifth Regiment was a part, attacked Bunker's Hill, which they took after a bayonet charge. The Regiment suffered 22 men killed and about 135 wounded. General Burgoyne wrote: "The Fifth has behaved the best, and suffered the most."[3]

- Middle of March 1776, the British Army, including the Fifth Regiment, embarked for Halifax, Nova Scotia, because it had no access to food and forage in Massachusetts and sufficient provisions could not be sent out from Britain. While in Halifax, the greater part of the troops remained aboard ship, because there were no quarters ashore for them. The Fifth remained in Halifax about two months.

- 3 Jul 1776, the Regiment made a landing on Staten Island, where it remained until reinforcements of British and Hessian troops arrived [from Europe].

- 22 Aug 1776, the Regiment descended on the southwest end of Long Island and had a successful skirmish with the rebels on 27 August. The Americans abandoned Brooklyn on 28 August, passing their troops across the East River to New York (Manhattan).

- 15 Sep 1776, the Fifth Regiment made a landing on New York Island (Manhattan) within a few miles of the city, and the Americans retreated to the northern end of the island.

- 28 Oct 1776, the Fifth formed part of an expedition to march on the American camp at White Plains. They were repulsed with little loss. The army retired to camps near the North River at Fordham Heights.

- 16 Nov 1776, the Fifth participated in a storming party to capture Fort Washington. A few days later it was detached across the North River against Fort Lee on the New Jersey shore of the Hudson River and thereafter took an active part in the reduction of New Jersey, being encamped first at English Neighborhood and thereafter at Maidenhead (by the early part of January 1777).

- 30 Jun 1777, the Regiment embarked for Staten Island, because forage could not be obtained in New Jersey excepting by skirmishing. A general engagement with the enemy was impossible, because "the enemy kept in the mountain fastnesses, by which he succeeded in defeating the design of the British commander."[4]

- 5 Jul 1777, the Regiment embarked at Sandy Hook, sailed to Chesapeake Bay, proceeded up the Elk River, landed at Elk Ferry on 25 August, and advanced on Philadelphia. The Americans took up position at Brandywine Creek to oppose the advance.

- 11 Sep 1777, British forces, including the Fifth Regiment, attacked the Americans at Chad's Ford, suffering some casualties but winning the field.

- 4 Oct 1777, the Regiment participated in the engagement at Germantown with considerable casualties.

- 18 Oct 1777, the Regiment removed from Germantown and encamped in the immediate vicinity of Philadelphia. In the meanwhile, the Americans formed a strong camp at White Marsh, fourteen miles from Philadelphia. During early December the Fifth took part in several skirmishes designed to bring on a general engagement, but the Americans could not be provoked, so on 8 December the Regiment returned to Philadelphia. In Philadelphia "the British lay in comfortable quarters ... where the want of strict discipline during the period of a temporary repose produced several evil consequences, particularly the estrangement of many persons previously in the interest of the royal cause."[5]

- 18 Jun 1778, as a consequence of France's joining the war on the American side, the British felt it necessary to retreat overland from Philadelphia to New York. The British Army units crossed the Delaware River on 18 June, proceeded through the Jerseys, with the Americans harassing their flanks. No action of importance took place until 28 June at Freehold, New Jersey, where several members of the Fifth Regiment were killed.

- Beginning of July 1778, the Fifth Regiment reached Sandy Hook and embarked for New York, where it was encamped beyond the town.

- September 1778, part of the Regiment was detached on an expedition against Little Egg Harbor, New Jersey, a noted rendezvous for privateers. The expeditionary force destroyed the town and proceeded 20 miles up the river to Chesnut Neck and returned.

- 3 Nov 1778, the Regiment sailed from Sandy Hook as part of the British expedition to capture the French West Indies.

Eight muster rolls covering the period 1774-1778, when the Fifth Regiment was active on the North American continent, are to be found in the Public Record Office, London, in a vast corpus of records designated War Office 12. All eight rolls are in volume 2289 at the pages cited.

Muster Roll	Where Prepared	Date	Volume 2289 Page Citation
A	Boston, MA	16 Jan 1775	152-162
B	Staten Island, Blazing Star	11 Jul 1776	164-169, 172
C	Rareton [Raritan?] Landing	23 Apr 1777	171, 175-180
D	Brunswick, NJ	22 Apr 1777	181
E	Philadelphia	08 Mar 1778	182, 184-187, 189-193, 196, 198-201
F	Philadelphia	23 Feb 1778	183, 197
G	Philadelphia	06 Feb 1778	188, 195
H	Staten Island	20 Jul 1778	202-211

Deserters

A number of Germans must have been recruited into the Fifth Regiment. One may hypothesize that British and German soldiers would have defected selectively as opportunity for slipping away from the main body of troops arose. Defections of British soldiers could have occurred at any time or place during the five years the Regiment was in North America, but German soldiers may have reasoned that, because there were few German settlers in New England, deserters would not find a hospitable welcome from the American populace. The German settlements of rural eastern Pennsylvania, on the other hand, would have welcomed them. The following table appears to bear out this hypothesis.

British Soldiers

Where Defecting	Year	Number
Near Boston	1774	14
Halifax, Nova Scotia, or Staten Island	1776	2*
At Philadelphia	1777	2*
	1778	10
Philadelphia or southern New Jersey	1778	3
Northern New Jersey	1778	1

German Soldiers

Where Defecting	Year	Number
Near Boston	1774	1
At Philadelphia	1777	3
	1778	5
Northern New Jersey	1777	4
	1778	1

*In each case, one soldier recaptured by the British.

Dischargees

A similar analysis of discharges from the Fifth Regiment is presented in the following table. It may be that the English-speaking dischargees were required to settle in Canada, most likely in Nova Scotia, rather than in the rebel colonies, despite the place where the actual mustering-out occurred. On the other hand, the two German dischargees, both mustered out in Philadelphia, might have been allowed to join their ethnic group in eastern Pennsylvania. In fact, however, we do not know what the British policy was for the settlement of men discharged from the army. We do know, however, that many soldiers were given land in Nova Scotia after 1783 for their services to the British forces during the American Revolution.

Where Discharged	Year	Number
Northern New Jersey	1776	1
	1777	12
Halifax, Nova Scotia, or Staten Island	1776	5
Long Island	1776	1
Boston, MA	1776	2
Philadelphia or southern New Jersey	1777	2
	1778	7*

*Includes two German soldiers discharged.

Prisoners of War

With regard to the prisoners of war listed hereinafter, nothing whatsoever is known. No doubt they were still interned when the Fifth Regiment left North America for the West Indies in 1778. Left behind, they had no troop unit to return to at the end of hostilities in 1783, and one can guess that these men remained in the United States, given the probability that no record existed of their prisoner of war status and the likelihood that the British Army commanders would have examined them on suspicion of desertion had they later returned after the war.

The letter or letters following each entry pertain to the muster roll citations, as listed above.

ACHESON, Thomas, deserted 19 Jun 1774, A

ALEXANDER, Thomas, p.o.w., B

ALLEN, Thomas, deserted 30 Aug 1774, A

BARKER, William, discharged 4 May 1778, H

BAUMER, John,[6] deserted 30 July 1774, A

BAXTER, Edward, discharged 23 Feb 1777, C

BAXTER, George, discharged 23 Feb 1777, E

BENHARD, George,[6] deserted 28 Nov 1777, E

BERGMYER [BERGMEIER?], Daniel,[6] deserted 20 Jun 1778, H

BLAKELY, William, deserted 12 May 1776 (returned), C

BOYLE, Henry, p.o.w., E; H

BREMER, Christian,[6] discharged 5 May 1777 or 1778, H

BRIGGS, George, discharged 5 May 1777 or 1778, H

BROOKS, George, deserted 3 Aug 1774, A

BROWN, Zachariah, p.o.w., E; H

BROWNE, William, deserted 28 May 1778, H

BULL?, George, deserted 6 Oct 1774, A

CLEMENTS, James, deserted 13 July 1774, A

CUBELAR [KUEBLER?], John,[6] discharged 5 May 1778, H

DAVIDSON, JONATHAN, discharged 2 Jun 1776, B

DAVIES, William, deserted 2 Jun 1776, B

DAVIS, William, p.o.w., C

DUNN, Carroll, sergeant, discharged 8 Jul 1776, B

EDMONDS, John, p.o.w., E; H

EDMONDS, Thomas, p.o.w., E

ERHART, Frederick,[6] p.o.w., E

ERHART, John,[6] p.o.w., H

ETZELL, John,[6] deserted 16 Jun 1778, H

FLOYD. See HOYD/HOYDE

FRANKLIN, William, deserted 19 Dec 1774, A

GEORGE, Jacob, p.o.w., D; F; H

GREEN, Dennis, p.o.w., B; C

GREEN, William, sergeant, discharged 7 Jul 1776, B

HARKINS, Charles, deserted 24 Jul 1774, A

HARRIS(S), Francis, discharged 23 Feb 1777, C; E

HEFLING [HOEFLING?], George,[6] deserted 20 Mar 1778, H

HICKEY, Thomas, discharged 23 Feb 1777 or 12 Apr 1777, C; E

HIGGINS, Thomas, deserted 24 Oct 1777 (returned), E; deserted second time 10 Apr 1778, H

HILL, Richard, discharged 23 Feb 1777, C

HOLTSMAN [HOLTZMANN?], Michael,[6] deserted 28 Nov 1777, E

HOMYER [HOHMEIER? HOCHMEIER?], George,[6] deserted 24 Feb 1777, C; E

HOYD? (or HOYDE), John, discharged 23 Feb 1777, C; E

HUBERT, Michael,[6] deserted 16 Jun 1777 or 1778, H

JAMES, John, deserted 4 Jul 1778, H

JONES, Joseph, p.o.w., H

KENADEY, John, deserted 16 Aug 1774, A

KIETH, James, deserted 20 Mar 1778, H

KIRSHNER [KIRSCHNER?], Philip,[6] deserted 22 or 23 Nov 1777, E

KNIEBEL or KNOEBEL. See NEABLE

LEBECK or LEEBECK [LUEBECK?], Anthony,[6] deserted 24 Feb 1777, C

LEEMAN [LEHMANN?], Diedrick,[6] deserted 20 Jun 1778, H

LEGFORD?, John, deserted 23 Mar 1778, H

LINE, Thomas, discharged 7 Jun 1776, A

McCOLLUM, John, deserted 27 Nov 1774, A

McKENZIE, James, p.o.w., E; H

McMAHAN, --?, deserted 31 Aug 1774, A

MAGEE, George, deserted 27 Nov 1774, A

MARSHMAN, Jeremiah, discharged 25 Dec 1776 or 1777, E

MASLIN, Robert, p.o.w., E; H

MEREDITH, David, discharged 23 Feb 1777, C

MILLER, James, p.o.w., G

MILLIGAN, George, discharged 23 Feb 1777, C; E

MOORE, George, discharged 7 Jun 1776, B

MOSELY, George, p.o.w., E; H

MOSELEY, John, p.o.w., F

NEABLE [KNIEBEL? KNOEBEL?], Christian,[6] deserted 20 Jun 1778, H

OSBORNE, William, discharged 5 May 1778, H

PATTISON, George, discharged 24 Jul 1777, E

PERRY, Benjamin, discharged 7 Jun 1776, B

PLUCKNETT, John, deserted 27 Jun 1778, H

PLUNKETT, Abraham, deserted 29 Jul 1774, A

POWER, William, discharged 24 Aug 1776, C

REEVES, William, discharged 23 Feb 1777, C

RICHMOND, James, deserted 10 Apr 1778, H

RIGGS, William, deserted 3 Aug 1774, A

ROSE, Robert, deserted 5 Mar 1778, H

ROSS, David, p.o.w., B; C; E

SHAUGHNESSY, Michael, deserted 13 Apr 1778, H

SHERIDEN, John, discharged 23 Feb 1777, E

SHINYMAN [SCHEINEMANN?], Frederick,[6] deserted 19 May 1777 or 1778, H

SMITH, Thomas, deserted 13 Apr 1778, H

SPENCER, Thomas, p.o.w., G; H

STALL [STAHL?], John,[6] deserted 19 May 1778, H

STEVENS, John, corporal, p.o.w., C; E; H

STORKE [STORCH?], William,[6] p.o.w., E; H

STUART, Alexander, discharged 23 Feb 1777, C; E

SULLIVAN, Daniel, discharged 7 Jun 1776, B

SULLIVAN, John, p.o.w., C; deserted 2 Sep 1777, E

SWENY, Francis, deserted 16 Aug 1774, A

TAYLOR, Dimock, discharged 7 Jun 1776, B

TAYLOR, Simon, deserted 14 Mar 1778, H

TAYLOR Thomas, deserted 16 Jun 1778, H

TILLEY, Robert, discharged 26 May 1777, E

WALSH, William, p.o.w., D; F; H

WATTS, Daniel, discharged 23 Feb 1777, C; E

WEST Jonathan, discharged 24 Jun 1778, H

WHITE, John, discharged 5 May 1778, H

WILSON, Thomas, discharged 25 Feb 1777 or 24 Jul 1777, E

---

1. Historical Record of the Fifth Regiment of Foot or Northumberland Fusiliers, Containing an Account of the Formation of the Regiment in the year 1674, and of Its Subsequent Services to 1837. Prepared for publication under the direction of the Adjutant General (London: W. Clowes & Sons, 1838), p. 39. This publication was not available in the British Museum when this writer sought to use it in 1976, but has been discovered in the Boston Public Library through the kind efforts of Dr. Robert Price of Lexington, Massachusetts, to whom this writer is indebted.

2. Ibid., p. 40.

3. Ibid., p. 43.

4. Ibid., p. 46.

5. Ibid., p. 47.

6. Probably a German.

III

DESERTERS, DISCHARGEES, AND PRISONERS OF WAR FROM THE SEVENTH REGIMENT OF FOOT (FUSILIERS)[1]

The Seventh Regiment of Foot, characterized by General Benedict Arnold as a weak regiment because it was largely composed of recruits more or less unwilling, many of whom probably had been shanghaied into service in England. In May 1775 the Regiment was one of only two units defending Canada. Sometime in the 1775-1777 period the Regiment was transported to New York, where it became part of the British expeditionary force assigned to quell the rebellion. The day-by-day orderly books of the Regiment, which might give us the details of this transfer, have not been seen by this writer, although they may possibly be found in the Royal Fusiliers Museum in the Tower of London. The Regiment fought in the following engagements:

06 Oct 1777   Participated in the capture of Fort Montgomery, as part of the rear guard.

26 Dec 1779   Sailed with Clinton on 26 Dec 1779 to capture Charleston. Arrived at the end of January 1780 at Tybee in Georgia. The fleet then sailed northward to John's Island and then to James' Island (Fort Johnston). Charleston surrendered on 9 May 1780. The Regiment then participated in skirmishes with the rebels inland from Charleston.

07 Jan 1781   The Regiment, under the command of Colonel Banastre Tarleton, was part of about 4,000 men who accompanied General Cornwallis in his advance northward from Charleston.

17 Jan 1781 Tarleton overtook the American force under General Daniel Morgan at Cowpens, where the Seventh Regiment was almost entirely captured.

Thus it was that the men of the Seventh Regiment came to have the opportunity to remain in the United States, and the evidence is that a great many of them did so. Most of them, through the happenstance of their capture at Cowpens, probably settled in the Carolinas.

Possibly because of the unreliability of the Regiment, it was mustered frequently; no less than thirty musters have been preserved in the Public Record Office, London, under War Office 12, volumes 2474 and 2475, covering the relevant years. Despite this plethora of data, there exist several obvious gaps in their sequence, with the consequence that crucial entries may have been lost for some of the men reported as prisoners of the rebels, deserters, or otherwise separated from the Regiment. The muster rolls preserved are as follows:

Place	Date	W.O. 12 Citation (Vol.:Page)
Canada	1772-1775	missing
01. Staten Island	19 May 1777	2474:255-264
02. York Island	24 May 1777	:270
03. Philadelphia	24 Apr 1778	:275-280
04. Philadelphia	23 Feb 1778	:281
05. Philadelphia	06 Feb 1778	:282
06. Philadelphia	24 Apr 1778	:283
07. Long Island	28 Jul 1778	:286-293
08. Southampton	23 Mar 1779	:295
09. New York Island	24 Dec 1778	:297-300
10. New Utrecht, L.I.	01 Jan 1779	:301
11. New York Island	24 Dec 1778	:302-304
12. Staten Island	16 Sep 1779	:307-309
13. Camp near Bedford	10 Sep 1779	:310
14. Staten Island	16 Sep 1779	:311-312
15. Marston's Wharf	26 Oct 1782	:315-324
16. Charles Town	24 Jun 1780	:325
17. Marston's Whart	26 Oct 1782	:326-327
18. Camp near East Chester	17 Jul 1780	:328-329
19. Marston's Wharf	26 Oct 1782	:330-335
20. Brooklyn	31 Jan 1781	:336
21. Marston's Wharf	26 Oct 1782	:337-342
22. Marston's Wharf	26 Oct 1782	2475:001-007
23. New York	28 May 1783	:008
24. Marston's Wharf	26 Oct 1782	:009-030
25. New York	10 Jan 1783	:031-035
26. Gloucester	13 Feb 1783	:036
27. New York	10 Jan 1783	:037-040
28. Gloucester	14 Feb 1783	:041
29. New York	28 May 1783	:042
30. New York	28 Jun 1783	:043-052

Series continues with 1784 musters from Marlborough. The 1783 musters repeatedly state that active soldiers were forwarded to Halifax, Nova Scotia, and invalids were transported to Europe.

Thus, we do not have muster rolls indicating when the Regiment was transported to New York from Canada, and very few for the years 1780 and 1781. Clearly, the reason for the lack of information on the years 170-1781 has to do with the fact that many of the members of the units were in enemy hands. The lengthy muster lists, dated 26 Oct 1782 and prepared at Marson's Wharf (location not ascertained), are probably intended to summarize the personnel changes after 1779.

Since we do not know precisely when the Regiment was transferred from Canada to New York, we must assume that all desertions prior to the 19 May 1777 muster roll at Staten Island could have occurred in Canada. Indeed, it seems significant that 1777 desertions ceased entirely after January, perhaps indicating that the transfer occurred shortly after that time, when the St. Lawrence River became navigable. If so, it appears that there was a continuing desertion problem among the troops when stationed in Canada, only halted temporarily when the Regiment was transported to New York.

Analysis of desertion rates, as recorded on the thirty muster rolls, discloses the following:

DESERTIONS, 1775-1783

Mo.	1775	1776	1777	1778	1779	1780	1781	1782	1783
Jan		5	8						
Feb		2		1		1			
Mar		5	2		1	2			
Apr		5	2	2	4		1		
May		4	1	1	2		2	1	
Jun			2	5	3				55
Jul	1		1	4	1				
Aug	1				2		1		
Sep			1		1	3	1		
Oct	1		6			1			
Nov	9					1			
Dec	4	4		1		1	1	1	
	13	28	8	17	12	16	7	7	56

As will be seen, attrition through desertion continued during the years 1778-177, and one may assume that all of them occurred from Manhattan (New York Island), Staten Island, or Long Island, excepting for a few reported from a unit of the Regiment located at Philadelphia, or on a foray near Bedford [Connecticut?]. A great many of the desertions during 1780 may have taken place in the Carolinas, where the majority of the personnel was to be found under British command. Desertions in 1781 through May 1783 present a problem for the researcher: How could the regimental officers have been able to determine who had deserted during the period, if most of the soldiers were prisoners of war in the Carolinas? The evidence is that the New York headquarters did not, in fact, have certain information on these soldiers, for they carried many men on their rolls as "prisoners of the rebels" who, in June 1783, had also to be declared as deserters because they did not return to the Regiment after cessation of hostilities and who probably had long since settled down in America. As a consequence, it may be supposed that all desertions recorded during the 1781 through May 1783 period occurred among personnel still stationed in New York, perhaps a few among soldiers in Carolina who had ecaped capture at Cowpens and were still under the command of British officers. We also assume that all 55 men declared deserters in June 1783 were originally prisoners of war who elected to become deserter-immigrants settling in the Carolinas.

These assumptions are important to the genealogical researcher for, as has been found in other studies of the movements of deserter-immigrants, determination of the probable place of desertion likewise predicts the locality in which these men joined the general populace of this country. In other words, a British soldier deserting in the Carolinas or New York is likely to have settled in those general regions and to have appeared in the appropriate 1790 decennial census, from whence the researcher may begin to trace his, and his descendants', postwar movements in America.

Separations from the Regiment need also to be considered, for the muster rolls do not indicate their nature. It is likely that some of these separations were transfers to other British military units; it is also likely that personnel unfit for service were shipped back to England all during the war period. But it is also possible that some personnel separated formally from the regiment may have remained in this country, probably in New York. Separations occurred as follows:

SEPARATIONS, 1775-1783

Year	Number
1775	0
1776	0
1777	3
1778	5
1779	1
1780	8
1781	8
1782	40
1783	6
	71

Although it is not known whether the British commanders allowed personnel under their control to remain in America, there were some advantages to such a policy. If not returned to England, invalids and retirees collected no pensions for their services; thus there would have been a saving to the Exchequer by leaving them in America. Furthermore, there was always the possibility of buying one's freedom from the commanding officers. As a consequence, any of the separated soldiers could have remained in America; we simply lack sufficient information confidently to predict the fate of these dischargees.

Hereinafter follow the names of deserters, dischargees, and prisoners of war from the British Seventh Regiment of Foot. Numbers in brackets refer to the page numbers in the various muster rolls: pages between 255 and 342 will be found in War Office 12, volume 2474; pages between 1 and 52 in volume 2475 thereof. By using the page citations and comparing them with the table of muster rolls on the preceding page of this monograph, researchers can sometimes determine the likely area of desertion or internement.

ADAM(S), John, prisoner of the rebels [337]; discharged 15 Mar 1781 [323; 337]

ADDAIR, John, deserted 5 May 1779? [327]; deserted 5 May 1780 [316]

ALBISON, John, prisoner [2]

ALLEN, Thomas, prisoner of the rebels [23]

ANDREWS, John, deserted 27 Nov 1775 [260]

ARBIGE, John. See John HARBIGE; HARBRIDGE

ARNOLD, George, prisoner of the rebels [8, 16, 24, 42]

ASHBY, William, prisoner of the rebels [320, 330, 335, 3, 12, 29, 40; [declared] deserter 16 Jun 1783 [52]

ATKINS, Edward, prisoner of the rebels [320, 330, 335, 3, 12, 29, 40]; [declared] deserter 16 Jun 1783 [52]

ATTAWAY (or AUTHAWAY), Thomas, prisoner of the rebels [339, 6, 18, 31]. See also Thomas HOLLOWAY

AVERY, Thomas, prisoner of the rebels [317, 325, 341, 9, 13, 26, 33]

AVOTT, John, prisoner of the rebels {322, 326, 342, 7, 17, 23, 34]; [declared] deserter [49]

BAILLIE, Edward, corporal, prisoner of the rebels [331, 334, 2, 11, 30, 37]

BAKER, William, deserted 23 Dec 1780 [315, 332, 333]

BANNER, John, prisoner of the rebels [7, 23, 34]

BARKER, Jonathan, discharged 25 Dec 1782 [38, 43]

BARROW? (BURROW?), Josiah, deserted 5 Jul 1779 [308]

BARTHOLOMEW, Robert, prisoner of the rebels [10, 15]

BARTHOLOMEW, Thomas, prisoner of the rebels [22]

BATTLE, James, prisoner of the rebels [37]

BATTLE, John, prisoner of the rebels [319, 331, 334, 2, 11, 30]

BELL, Richard, prisoner of the rebels [4]

BELL, Robert, prisoner of the rebels [321, 324, 338, 14, 28, 38]; [declared] deserter 16 Jun 1783[43]

BELTON, James, prisoner of the rebels [337, 10, 15]

BENDALL, Nicholas, prisoner of the rebels [341, 9, 13, 33]

BIBB, William, prisoner of the rebels [8, 16, 24, 42]; [declared] deserter 16 Jun 1783 [47]

BIGGS, Joseph, deserted 18 Feb 1776 [261]

BILTON (also BILLON), James, prisoner of the rebels [318, 323, 22, 35]; [declared] deserter 16 Jun 1783 [48]

BLACKLOCK, John, sergeant, prisoner of the rebels [7, 17, 23, 34]

BLAKER, John, deserted 24 Nov 1775 [255]

BLASDELL, Thomas, deserted 5 Apr 1776 [263]

BLUNDEN, Thomas, deserted 24 Dec 1775 [258]

BONNER, John, prisoner [17]

BOSKETT, John, deserted 20 Apr 1776 [262]

BOUCH, James, corporal, prisoner of the rebels [321, 338, 4, 14, 38]

BOWEL, Thomas, deserted 10 Oct 1778 [299]

BOWERS, William, discharged 20 Aug 1782 [41]

BOY, Joseph, discharged 24 Nov 1778 [300]

BRITTAIN, William, discharged 25 Dec 1782 [38, 43]

BROOKS, Joseph, deserted 10 Oct 1778 [299]

BROUGHTON, John, prisoner of the rebels [280]

BROWN, John, deserted 21 Jun 1778 [286]

BROWN, Richard, deserted 4 Jan 1776 [262]

BROWN, Thomas, deserted 8 Jan 1777 [259]

BROWN, William, corporal, prisoner of the rebels [315, 332, 333, 1, 20, 21, 39]

BUGG, John, discharged 21 Jan 1783 [48]

BUNGY, Joshua, prisoner of the rebels [29, 40]

BUNTING, Thomas, deserted 27 Nov 1775 [259]

BURK, Ulick, discharged 25 Dec 1782 [35]; possibly a German

BURR, John, discharged 11 Jun 1783 [50]

BURROW? (BARROW?), Josiah, deserted 5 Jul 1779 [308]

BURT, Nicholas, prisoner of the rebels [12, 29, 40]; [declared] deserter [52]

BURTON, Isaac, prisoner of the rebels [333, 1, 21, 39]; deserted 16 Nov 1781 [315]

BURTON, James, [declared] deserter 16 Jun 1783 [50]

CALDWELL, Henry, sergeant, prisoner of the rebels [338, 4, 14, 38]

CALLOW, Thomas, sergeant, prisoner of the rebels [21]

CAMPION, John, discharged 21 Mar 1782 [22]

CANNON, Michael, deserted 4 Apr 1779? [328]; discharged 16 Oct 1782 [32]

CARDER, Isaac, discharged 23 Feb 1780 [315, 332]

CARMACK, Peter, discharged 25 Dec 1782 [32, 45]

CARR, John, sergeant, prisoner of the rebels [13, 26]

CARR, William, sergeant, prisoner of the rebels [3, 12, 29, 40]

CARTER, George, discharged 24 Feb 1780? [332]

CAVE, John, sergeant, prisoner of the rebels [33]

CHACE, James, separated 15 Mar 1781 [337]. See also James CHASE

CHALLINER (CHALLINOR; CHANNILER), George, prisoner of the rebels [10, 15, 22]

CHANDLER, George, prisoner of the rebels [35]

CHANNILER, George. See George CHALLINER

CHARLES, Joseph, deserted 31 May 1779? [328]

CHASE, James, deserted 5 Jul 1779 [309]. See also James CHACE

CLARKE, B. R., discharged 31 Mar 1782 [20, 21]

CLARKE, Thomas, deserted 22 Apr 1778 [275]

CLAYTON, Robert, prisoner of the rebels [317, 325, 341, 9, 13, 26, 33]

CLEMENS (CLEMENTS; CLEMMENS), Richard, drummer, prisoner of the rebels [315, 332, 333, 1, 20, 21, 39]; [declared] deserter 16 Jun 1783 [50]

CLUFF, John, prisoner of the rebels [334, 2, 11, 30]

COOK, Edward, deserted 19 Sep 1781 [3, 12]

COOK, William, Senior, prisoner of the rebels [322, 326, 342, 7, 17, 23, 34]; [declared] deserter 16 Jun 1783 [49]

COOPER, Edward, discharged 30 Mar 1780 [327]; discharged 21 Apr 1780 [316]

COOPLAND (or COPELAND), John, prisoner of the rebels [6, 18, 27, 31]; [declared] deserter 16 Jun 1783 [44]

COSCOMB, Thomas, prisoner, [323]. See also Thomas GOSCOMB

COYLE (or COYLES), Thomas, prisoner of the rebels [323, 337, 10, 15, 22, 35]

CRAFT (or CROFT), Thomas, prisoner of the rebels [7, 17, 23, 34]; [declared] deserter 16 Jun 1783 [49]

CROPER, Thomas, deserted 25 Jan 1776 [255]

CROSS, Noah, deserted 27 Jan 1776 [264]

CROW, Charles, prisoner of the rebels [319, 331, 334, 2, 11, 30, 37]

CROWLEY, Cornelius, prisoner of the rebels [321, 324, 338, 4, 28, 38]

CROWLEY, James, prisoner of the rebels [319, 331, 334, 11, 30, 37]; [declared] deserter 16 Jun 1783 [51]

CURTICE (or CURTIS), Edward, prisoner of the rebels [339, 6, 18, 31]

CURTICE, Richard?, prisoner of the rebels [27]

CUSHNER, Alexander, prisoner of the rebels [32]; probably German, if so, correctly KIRSCHNER

DABNEY? William, prisoner of the rebels [16]

DANDY, John, prisoner of the rebels [342, 7, 17, 23]

DAVIS, Benjamin, prisoner of the rebels [322, 326, 342, 7, 23, 17, 23]

DAVIS, David, deserted 17 Nov 1776 [261]

DAVIS, Robert, deserted 11 Jun 1783 [50]

DAVIS, Thomas, prisoner [333]

DAWSON, Thomas, prisoner of the rebels [331, 334, 2, 11, 30, 37]

DAY, James, deserted 21 Jan 1777 [264]

DESPARD (also DEPRARD), John, captain, prisoner on parole [318, 337, 10, 15, 22]

DICKENS (also DICKINGS, DICKINS), John, corporal, prisoner of the rebels [334, 2, 11, 30, 37]

DINGLEY, Thomas, prisoner of the rebels [341, 9, 13, 26, 33]

DORSON, Thomas, prisoner [319]

DOWLING, Jeremiah, discharged 7 Oct 1778 [304]

DOWNEY, William, prisoner of the rebels [8, 24, 42]

DUDDEN, William, deserted 15 Nov 1775 [257]. See also William DUTTEN

DUGMORE, Josiah, deserted 21 Jan 1777 [255]

DUNN, Thomas, prisoner on parole [34]

DUTTEN, William, deserted 20 Mar 1776 [257]. See also William DUDDEN

EAGLE, Edward, prisoner of the rebels [320, 330, 335, 3, 12, 29, 40]; [declared] deserter 16 Jun 1783 [52]

EASTHAM, George, deserted 30 May 1783 [45]

EATON, George, separated 25 Dec 1782 [31, 44]

EDMONDS, Charles, prisoner of the rebels [321, 324, 338, 4, 14, 28, 38]; [declared] deserter [43]

EDWARDS, John, corporal, prisoner of the rebels [337, 10, 15, 22]

ENDELL (or ENDLE), John, prisoner of the rebels [8, 16, 24, 42]; [declared] deserter 16 Jun 1783 [47]; possibly a German

EVELEIGH, William, discharged 23 Feb 1780 [322, 326]

EWER (or EWRE), William, prisoner of the rebels [321, 324, 338, 4, 28, 38]

FALLARD, Tobias. See Thomas FOLLARD

FILING (also FILLING, FOYLINGS, FYLING), Peter, [6, 8, 27, 31, 42]; [declared] deserter 16 Jun 1783 [44]; possibly a German, if so, probably PFEILING or PFEULING

FISHBACK, Francis, discharged 23 Feb 1782 [10,22]; probably a German

FITZGARROLD (or FITZGERALD), William, deserted 10 Oct 1780 [315, 332, 333]

FLOWER, John, deserted 10 Mar 1776 [262]

FLUCK, William, prisoner of the rebels [342, 7, 17, 23, 34, 42]

FOLLARD, Tobias, prisoner of the rebels [8, 16, 24, 42]; [declared] deserter 16 Jun 1783 [47]

FORBES, Henry, discharged 24 Nov 1778 [300]

FORREST, Alexander, deserted 1 May 1776 [263]

FOX, James, prisoner of the rebels [317, 325, 341, 9, 13, 26]

FOX, Thomas, prisoner of the rebels [319, 331, 334, 2, 11, 30, 37]

FOYLINGS, Peter. See Peter FILING

FREEMAN, William, prisoner of the rebels [315, 332, 333, 1, 20, 21, 39]

FRICKETT, Japh.? [Joseph?], prisoner [326]. See also Joseph TRICKETT

FRISKIN, George, prisoner of the rebels [315, 332, 333, 1, 20, 21, 39]

FULLARD, Tobias. See Tobias FOLLARD

FYLING, Peter. See Peter FILING

GAHE? (GATE?), Thomas, deserted 1 May 1776 [263]

GALLAIHER, Patrick, deserted 19 Jun 1778 [293]

GARDENER (or GARDINER; GARDNER), John, prisoner of the rebels [315, 1, 20, 21, 39]; [declared] deserter 16 Jun 1783 [50]

GAREY (or GARY), Thomas, prisoner of the rebels [320, 330, 335, 3, 12, 40]; [declared] deserter 16 Jun 1783 [52]

GARRATT, Andrew, [declared] deserter 16 Jun 1783 [47] see also Andrew JARRATT

GARRATT, William, prsioner of the rebels [316, 327, 339, 6, 18, 27, 31]

GARY, Thomas. See Thomas GAREY

GASCOMB, Thomas, prisoner [318]; see also Thomas GOSCOMB

GATE, Thomas. See Thomas GAHE

GENTLE, Edward, discharged 25 Dec 1782 [38]

GILES, William, prisoner of the rebels [8, 16, 24, 42]

GILLMAN (or GILMAN), Francis (or Frances), prisoner of the rebels [29, 40]

GLOVER, Richard, discharged 25 Dec 1782 [48]

GORDON, John, deserted 30 May 1783 [45]

GOSCOMB, (or COSCOMB, GASCOMB) Thomas, prisoner of the rebels [318, 323, 337, 10, 15, 22, 35]

GRACE, Thomas, prisoner of the rebels [324, 338, 4, 14, 28, 38]

GRACE, William, prisoner of the rebels [40]; see also William GROCE

GRAY, James, prisoner of the rebels [3, 12, 29, 40]

GRAY, Thomas, prisoner of the rebels [29]

GREEN, Clem, prisoner of the rebels [2, 11, 30]; see also Clem GRISSEN

GREEN, Daniel, discharged 25 Dec 1782 [35]

GREEN, Edward, deserted 20 Feb 1780 [329]

GREEN, Samuel, discharged 25 Dec 1782 [31, 44]

GREGORY, Philip, deserted 23 Nov 1775 [260]

GRIFFIN, John, corporal, prisoner of the rebels [325, 341, 9, 13, 26, 33]

GRIFFIN, Timothy, deserted 6 Feb 1778 [283]; deserted 25 Jun 1779 [307]

GRIMES, James, deserted 2 Mar 1780 [322, 326]

GRISSEN? Clem, prisoner [334]; see also Clem GREEN

GROCE, William, prisoner of the rebels [330, 335, 3, 12, 29]; see also William GRACE

GROW, William, prisoner [320]

HALL, Thomas, prisoner of the rebels [7, 17, 23, 34]

HAMILTON, John, deserted 11 Oct 1778 [297]

HARBIGE (also ARBIGE, HARBRIDGE, HARBRIGE), John, prisoner of the rebels [341, 9, 13, 26, 33]

HARDING, John, drummer, deserted 26 Jan 1776 [260]

HARDY, George, prisoner of the rebels [330, 3, 12, 29]

HARGROVE, Christopher, deserted 12 Apr 1782 [318, 323]

HARRIS (or HARRISS), John, prisoner of the rebels [318, 323, 337, 10, 15, 22, 35]

HARRIS, William, deserted 11 Oct 1778 [302]

HARRISON, John, prisoner of the rebels [38]

HARRISON, Joseph, prisoner of the rebels [4, 14, 28]

HARRISON, Joshua (or Josiah), prisoner of the rebels [321, 324, 338]

HARRISS, John. See John HARRIS

HART, William, prisoner of the rebels [321, 324, 338, 4, 14, 28, 38]; [declared] deserter 16 Jun 1783 [43]

HARVEY, William, prisoner of the rebels [9]

HAWKENS, Thomas, deserted 14 Jul 1779 [307]

HAWORTH, James, prisoner of the rebels [3, 12]; see also James HOWARTH, HOWORTH

HAYS, James, discharged 25 Dec 1782 [40]; discharged 23 Feb 1783 [52]

HAZEL (or HAZLE, HEAZEL), Benjamin, prisoner of the rebels [321, 324, 338, 4, 28, 38]

HEARD, John, discharged 21 Jan 1783 [44]

HEARD, William, discharged 21 Jan 1783 [44]

HEATH, Henry, prisoner [255]

HEAZEL, Benjamin. See Benjamin HAZEL

HEBERY (or HIBERY), John, prisoner of the rebels [318, 323, 337, 10, 15, 22, 35]

HICKS, Thomas, prisoner of the rebels [315, 332, 333, 1, 20, 21, 39]

HILL, George, deserted 9 Jun 1779 [308]

HILL, Thomas, prisoner of the rebels [337, 10, 15, 22, 35]

HILSON (or HILTON), John, prisoner of the rebels [341, 9, 13, 26, 33]

HODGES, Thomas, prisoner of the rebels [317, 325, 341, 9, 13, 26, 33]

HOGAN, Michael, prisoner of the rebels [322, 326, 342, 7, 17, 23, 34]

HOLDEN, William, deserted 25 Dec 1781 [8, 16, 24]

HOLLOWAY, Thomas, discharged 25 Dec 1782 [48]; see also Thomas ATTAWAY

HOOKER, Henry, discharged 25 Dec 1781 [322, 326, 342, 7, 17, 23]

HOOPER, Samuel, deserted 16 May 1782 [2, 11]

HORNER, Joseph, deserted 9 Jun 1779 [308]

HORTON, George, prisoner of the rebels [9, 13, 26]

HOWARTH, George, sergeant, discharged 23 Feb 1780 [324]

HOWARTH (or HOWORTH), James, prisoner of the rebels [320, 330, 335, 29, 40]; see also James HAWORTH

HUDSON, John, discharged 25 Dec 1782 [38]

HUGHES (or HUGHS), Charles, prisoner of the rebels [322, 326, 342, 7, 17, 23, 34]

HUGHES, John, corporal, discharged 24 Feb 1782 [13, 26]

HUGHES, Johnson, deserted 2 Oct 1782 [32]

HUGHS, Charles. See Charles HUGHES

HULL, Richard, deserted 3 Nov 1776 [261]

HUNT, Edmund, discharged 23 Aug 1782 [36]

HUSBAND (or HUSBANDS), Charles, discharged 23 Feb 1780 [322, 326]

HYNES, William, deserted 16 Jun 1780 [317, 325]

INGRAM, Henry, prisoner of the rebels [319, 331, 334, 2, 11, 30, 37]

IRWIN, Christopher, discharged 24 Feb 1779? [328]

JANES, John, [declared] deserter 16 Jun 1783 [46]; see also John JONES

JANNERY, John, discharged 25 Dec 1782 [31]

JARRATT, Andrew, prisoner of the rebels [8, 24, 42]; see also Andrew GARRATT

JEACH, William, corporal. See William LEACH

JEANES (or JEANS), John, prisoner of the rebels [217, 325, 341, 9, 13, 26, 33]

JEFFERY, Robert, prisoner of the rebels [319, 331, 334, 11, 30, 37]

JENKINS, John, corporal, prisoner of the rebels [3, 12, 29, 40]

JOHNSON, Joseph, discharged 23 Feb 1782 [1]

JONES, James, prisoner of the rebels [316, 327, 339, 6, 18, 27, 31]

JONES, John, prisoner of the rebels [318, 323, 339, 10, 15, 22, 35]

JONES, Richard, prisoner of the rebels [8, 16, 24, 42]; [declared] deserter 16 Jun 1783 [47]

JONES, Thomas, deserted 25 Mar 1776 [260]

JONES, William, deserted 10 Oct 1778 [297]

KELLEY (or KELLY), Daniel, discharged 23 Feb 1780 [317, 325]

KELLEY, James, deserted 6 Oct 1776 [261]

KENNEDY, William, discharged 25 Dec 1782 [33, 46]

KIRBY, Thomas, discharged 24 Nov 1778 [301]

KIRSCHNER, Alexander. See Alexander CUSHNER

KNOWLES, James (or Joshua), sergeant, prisoner of the rebels [337, 10, 15, 22, 35]

KYRIE? Robert, corporal. See Robert RYRIE

LACKE, William, [declared] deserted 16 Jun 1783 [43]

LAMBOURN, Thomas, prisoner of the rebels [9]

LANDER, John, prisoner of the rebels [318, 323, 337, 10, 15, 22, 35]; [declared] deserter 16 Jun 1783 [48]

LANGFORD, John, prisoner of the rebels [10, 15, 22, 35]

LANGHAM, William, deserted 1 May 1776 [263]

LATTAMORE (or LATTERMORE, LATTIMORE), Richard, prisoner of the rebels [339, 6, 18, 31]; [declared] deserter 16 Jun 1783 [44]

LAVENDER, William, prisoner of the rebels [321, 324, 338, 4, 14, 28, 38]

LAVORY, Richard, prisoner [331]; see also SAVORY

LAW, Thomas, prisoner of the rebels [334, 2, 11, 29, 30, 37, 40]; [declared] deserter 16 Jun 1783 [51, 52]

LAWRENCE, Alfred, drummer, prisoner of the rebels [24, 42]

LEACH, William, corporal, prisoner of the rebels [339, 18, 27, 31]; [declared] deserter 16 Jun 1783 [44]

LEEDS, John, prisoner of the rebels [319, 331, 334, 2, 11, 30, 37]

LEISTER (or LESTER), James, prisoner of the rebels [8, 16, 24]; [declared] deserter 16 Jun 1783 [47]

LENAN (or LENNON, LENON), Thomas, discharged 24 Feb 1782 [321, 324, 338, 14, 28]; discharged 24 Jul 1782 [4]

LESTER, James. See James LEISTER

LESTER, Robert, discharged 24 Nov 1778 [300]

LIDDLE, Thomas, discharged 25 Dec 1782 [46]

LITTLEWOOD, Thomas, prisoner of the rebels [297]

LOCK (or LOCKE), William, prisoner of the rebels [341, 9, 13, 28, 38]

LODDY, James, prisoner of the rebels [7, 17, 23, 34]

LOMAX, John, discharged 25 Dec 1782 [34]; discharged 23 Feb 1783 [49]

LOMAX, Marsn?, discharged 25 Dec 1782 [21, 35]

LONG, William, corporal, prisoner of the rebels [39, 50]

LOVATT, Lovat, discharged 23 Feb 1782 [322, 326, 342, 7, 17, 23]

LOW, William, prisoner of the rebels [12]

LOW, Zachariah, deserted 24 Dec 1775 [263]

LUCAS, William, discharged 25 Dec 1782 [35]

MANNTLE? James, deserted 29 Apr 1780 [316]

MANSFIELD, Robert, corporal, prisoner of the rebels [334, 2, 11, 30, 37]; [declared] deserter 16 Jun 1783 [51]

MANUELL, James, deserted 29 Apr 1779? [327]

MARCHANT, William, deserted 27 Nov 1775 [259]

MARPLES, James, deserted 25 Nov 1775 [264]

MARRICK (or MARRICKS), John, prisoner of the rebels [20, 21]; see also John MERRICK, MEYRICK

MATHEWS (or MATTHEWS), William, prisoner of the rebels [315, 332, 333, 1, 20, 21, 39]

MAYCOCK, Thomas, corporal, prisoner of the rebels [6]

MAYERS, John, prisoner of the rebels [10, 15, 22, 35]; [declared] deserter 16 Jun 1783 [48]; probably a German; see also John MEARS

MAZIE? (MUZIE?), John. See John MEASY

McCLOUD, Alexander, prisoner of the rebels [318, 323, 337]

McDONALD, Donald, prisoner of the rebels [315, 332, 333, 1, 20, 21, 39]; [declared] deserter 16 Jun 1783 [50]

McDONALD, James, discharged 23 Jan 1782 [322, 326, 342, 7, 17, 23]

McDONAUGH, John, deserted 16 May 1782 [320, 330, 3, 12, 29]

McHIVER, Lacky. See Lacky McKIVER

McINTOSH, William, deserted 24 Jun 1779 [310]

McKIVER, Lacky, prisoner of the rebels [322, 326, 7, 23, 34]; [declared] deserter 16 Jun 1783 [49]

McLEOD, Alexander, prisoner of the rebels [10, 15, 22]

McLEOD, Donald, discharged 25 Dec 1782 [46]

McVICKER(S), Daniel, discharged 25 Dec 1782 [37]; discharged 23 Feb 1783 [51]

MEALING, John, prisoner of the rebels [38]; [declared] deserter 16 Jun 1783 [43]

MEALING, Richard, prisoner of the rebels [4, 14, 28]; see also Richard NEALING

MEANS, John, prisoner [318]

MEARS, John, prisoner of the rebels [323, 337]; see also John MAYERS

MEASEY (or MAZIE, MOSEY, MUZIE), John, prisoner of the rebels [339, 6, 18, 27, 31]

MEDLAM, William, deserted 4 Dec 1776 [264]

MEE, Benjamin, deserted 11 Dec 1775 [264]

MERCER (also MERAR), William, prisoner of the rebels [330, 3, 12, 40]

MERRICK (or MEYRICK), John, prisoner of the rebels [315, 332, 333, 1, 39]; see also John MARRICK(S)

MILES, Thomas, corporal, prisoner of the rebels [316, 327, 339, 6, 18, 27, 31]

MILLER, John, discharged 14 May 1777 [258]

MILLS, Samuel, deserted 20 Mar 1776 [263]

MITCHELL, Francis, deserted 4 Jul 1778 [290]; deserted 13 Feb 1780 [330]

MOON, Samuel, discharged 13 Nov 1781? [13]

MOOR, Samuel, deserted 13 Nov 1781 [9]; possibly the same as Samuel MOON

MORRIS, David, deserted 24 Sep 1780 [316]

MORRIS, John, prisoner of the rebels [8, 16, 24, 42]; [declared] deserted 16 Jun 1783 [47]

MORRIS, Thomas, deserted 31 May 1780 [318, 323]; deserted 5 Sep 1782 [36]

MORTON, John, corporal, prisoner of the rebels [335]

MORTON, William, prisoner of the rebels [7, 17, 23]

MOSEY, John. See John MEASEY

MULVEY, Jeremiah, deserted 6 Apr 1779? [327]; deserted 6 Apr 1780 [316]

MUMFORD, Stephen, prisoner of the rebels [317, 325, 341, 9, 13, 26, 33]

MURDOCH, James, deserted 7 Apr 1776 [255]

MURPHY, James, discharged 21 Jan 1783 [052]

MUZIE?, John. See John MEASEY

NEALING, Richard, prisoner of the rebels [338]; see also Richard MEALING

NEALY (or NELLEY), John, prisoner of the rebels [282]; deserted 19 Jul 1782? [32]

NELSON, James, deserted 26 Jan 1776 [260]

NEWELL, Henry, prisoner of the rebels [319, 331, 334, 2, 11, 30, 37]

NEWEY (or NEWY), Thomas, prisoner of the rebels [315, 332, 333, 1, 20, 21, 39]

NEWTON, James, discharged 25 Dec 1782 [38]

NEWY, Thomas. See Thomas NEWEY

NICHOLS, James, discharged 25 Dec 1782 [34]; discharged 23 Feb 1783 [49]

NORMAN, James, discharged 21 Jan 1783 [44]

ODELL, John, prisoner of the rebels [333, 1, 21, 39]

OWEN, John, prisoner of the rebels [320, 330, 335, 3, 12, 29, 40]; [declared] deserted 16 Jun 1783 [52]

PAIN, William, Senior, deserted 10 Dec 1776 [257]

PAINE, William, prisoner of the rebels [8, 16, 24, 42]; [declared] deserter 16 Jun 1783 [47]

PARKER (or PARKES), John, prisoner of the rebels [342, 7, 17, 23, 34]

PARKINSON, John, discharged 15 Mar 1781 [315, 332, 333]

PEARCE, Isaac, deserted 21 Jan 1777 [264]

PERCIVALL, Frances, discharged 16 Aug 1782 [41]

PERRYMAN, William, prisoner of the rebels [8, 16, 24, 42]; [declared] deserter 16 Jun 1783 [47]

PETERS, Joseph, prisoner of the rebels [8, 16, 24, 42]

PFEILING (or PFEULING), Peter. See Peter FILING

PHILLIPS, William, prisoner of the rebels [10, 15, 22, 35]

PIKE, John, prisoner of the rebels [316, 327, 339, 6, 18, 27, 31]; [declared] deserter 16 Jun 1783 [44]

PLAW, John, discharged 24 May 1777 [270]

POWEL, William, sergeant, discharged 15 Mar 1781 [6]

PRICE, John, prisoner of the rebels [38]

PRICE, Paul, deserted 21 Jan 1777 [263]

PRICE, Richard, prisoner of the rebels [338, 4, 14, 28]

PRIEST(T), Joseph, prisoner of the rebels [3, 12, 29]; [declared] deserter 16 Jun 1783 [52]

PRIEST, Robert, prisoner of the rebels [40]

RATHBONE, Benjamin, sergeant, discharged 24 Aug 1782 [45]

REED, James, deserted 9 Sep 1781 [320]

REED, John, deserted 9 Sep 1781 [330, 3, 12]

RENOLDS, Timothy. See Timothy REYNOLDS

REYNOLDS, James, prisoner of the rebels [317, 325, 341, 9, 13, 26, 33]

REYNOLDS (also RENOLDS), Timothy, prisoner of the rebels [334, 2, 11, 30, 37]; deserted 16 Mar or May 1782 [320, 330, 335, 3, 12, 29]

RICHARDS, William, deserted 5 Jun 1782? [323]

RICHARDSON, Thomas, deserted 21 Jan 1777 [258]

RICKET(T)S, Joseph, prisoner of the rebels [342, 7, 17, 23, 34

RIGLEY, William, discharged 15 Mar 1781 [315, 332, 1]

RIRIE, Robert. See Robert RYRIE

ROBERTSON, Thomas, deserted 28 Apr 1779 or 1780 [316, 327]

ROGERS, John, deserted 12 Apr 1779 or 1780 [316, 327]

ROGERS, Peter, sergeant, discharged 25 Dec 1782 [34]; discharged 23 Feb 1783 [49]

ROLLINGS, Richard, deserted 1 Dec 1776 [260]

ROWLAND, Edward, prisoner [335]; discharged 24 Feb 1782 [320, 330, 3, 12, 29]

ROWLAND, John, prisoner of the rebels [321, 324, 338, 4, 28, 38]

RUSTON, William, deserted 21 Jan 1777 [259]

RYAN, John, deserted 5 Jul 1779 [311]

RYDER, Thomas, prisoner of the rebels [1, 20, 21]

RYLEY, Mat(t)hew, discharged 23 Feb 1780 or 1781 [315, 332]

RYRIE, Robert, corporal, prisoner of the rebels [341, 9, 13, 26, 33]; [declared] deserter 16 Jun 1783 [46]

SANBIDGE, Thomas, discharged 3 Apr 1777 [257]

SAVAGE, Daniel, deserted 24 Mar 1778 [276]

SAVORY, Richard, prisoner of the rebels [319, 334, 2, 30, 37]; see also Richard LAVORY

SENNETT (or SENNITT), Patrick, discharged 25 Dec 1782 [31, 44]

SERGEANT, William, deserted 1 Dec 1776 [260]

SHARP, John, discharged 25 Dec 1782 [40]; discharged 23 Feb 1783 [52]

SHELTON, John, deserted 5 Dec 1778 [297]

SHORT (or SHORTO, SHORTTOE), Thomas, prisoner of the rebels [339, 6, 18, 27]

SIBLEY (or SIBLIE), John, prisoner of the rebels [320, 335, 3, 12, 29, 40]

SLATER, George, prisoner of the rebels [35]

SLATER, James, prisoner of the rebels [15, 22]

SLATER, John, prisoner of the rebels [10]

SLATER, Michael, prisoner [17]

SLATER, Richard, prisoner of the rebels [342, 7, 23, 34]; [declared] deserter 16 Jun 1783 [49]

SMALLWOOD, William, prisoner of the rebels [12, 29, 40]

SMITH, Daniel, sergeant, prisoner of the rebels [316, 327, 339, 6, 18, 27, 31]

SMITH, James, deserted 23 Mar 1778 [278]

SMITH, John, prisoner of the rebels [279]

SMITH, Richard, deserted 13 Dec 1775 [261]

SNODGRASS, William, deserted 6 Apr 1776 [264]

SPENCER, Thomas, prisoner of the rebels 19 Jan 1781 [336]

SPERWOOD, Timothy, discharged 15 Mar 1781 [6]

SPYCER (or SPYER), Francis, prisoner [321, 324]

STANISSTREET (STANISTREET, STANNESSTREET), Richard, prisoner of the rebels [321, 324, 338, 4, 14, 28, 28]; [declared] deserter 16 Jun 1783 [43]

STANLEY, Michael, prisoner of the rebels [318, 323, 337, 10, 15, 22, 35]

STANNESSTREET, Richard. See Richard STANISSTREET

STAR, James, corporal, deserted 27 Sep 1778 [295]

STEVENS, Alexander, prisoner of the rebels [321, 324, 338, 4, 14, 28, 38]

STEVENS, John, prisoner of the rebels [339, 6, 18, 27, 31]; [declared] deserter 16 Jun 1783 [44]

STEVENSON, John, ptisoner of the rebels [321, 338, 4, 14, 28, 38]; [declared] deserter 16 Jun 1783 [43]

STEVENSON, Thomas, prisoner [324]

STEWART, Alexander. See Alexander STUART

STONE, William, deserted 26 Aug 1776 [261]

STOVER? William, prisoner of the rebels [29]

STUART, Alexander, corporal, prisoner of the rebels [332, 333, 1, 20, 21, 39]

STUART, John, deserted 12 Jul 1776 [259]

SUCH, William, drummer, prisoner of the rebels [315, 332, 333, 337, 1, 10, 15, 20, 21, 22, 35, 39]

SUFFOLK, George, prisoner of the rebels [316, 327, 339, 6, 18, 27, 31]

SUNDERLAND, John, sergeant, prisoner of the rebels [334, 2, 11, 30, 37]

SUTHERLAND, Daniel, discharged 25 Dec 1782 [35]

SYMONDS, Ephraim, sergeant, discharged 19 Mar 1782 [13, 28]

TALBOT(T), Charles, prisoner of the rebels [318, 323, 337, 10, 15, 22, 35]; [declared] deserter 16 Jun 1783 [48]

TAYSON, Timothy, prisoner of the rebels [334, 2, 11, 30]

TERNAN (or TERNON), Hugh, prisoner of the rebels [8, 16, 24, 42]; [declared] deserter 16 Jun 1783 [47]

TERRAL, William, deserted 14 Oct 1778 [295]

THOMAS, John, prisoner of the rebels [42]

THOMPSON, John, prisoner of the rebels [317, 325, 341, 9, 13, 28, 38]; [declared] deserter 16 Jun 1783 [43]

THORNHILL, Peter, prisoner [341]

THORNTON, George, prisoner of the rebels [318, 323, 337, 10, 15, 22, 35]

TIBBISH, Francis, discharged 23 Feb 1782 [323, 337, 15]

TIBBISH, Imanuel?, discharged 23 Jul? 1782 [318]; [perhaps 23 Feb 1782 is meant; see Francis TIBBISH]

TILFORD, Adam, deserted 21 Jan 1777 [257]

TIMMIS, Thomas, deserted 25 Mar 1776 [but] returned [260]

TINKLER (or TINKLEY), William, corporal, prisoner of the rebels [337, 10, 15, 22, 35]

TINNERY? John, discharged 25 Dec 1782 [44]

TONG (or TONGUE), William, prisoner of the rebels [332, 333, 1, 20, 39]

TOWERS, Dennis, discharged [33, 46]

TRICKETT, James, prisoner of the rebels [7, 17, 23, 34]; [declared] deserter 16 Jun 1783 [49]

TRICKETT(S), Joseph, prisoner of the rebels [322, 342]; see also Japh? [Joseph?] FRICKETT

TUCKER, Thomas, prisoner of the rebels [316, 327, 339, 6, 18, 27, 31]

TURNER, Robert, prisoner of the rebels [333, 1, 20, 21, 39]; [declared] deserter 16 Jun 1783 [50]

UNDERHILL, Henry, deserted 7 Apr 1776 [264]

UNDERHILL, Henry, discharged 7 Mar 1782 [22]

VICKERS, John, prisoner of the rebels [10, 1, 22, 35]

VINCENT, John, deserted 22 Apr 1778 [275]

WALKER, William, prisoner of the rebels [8, 16, 24, 42]

WARD, George, discharged 25 Dec 1782 [33, 46]

WARDELL, John, discharged 25 Dec 1782 [31, 44]

WARDER, Henry, prisoner of the rebels [319, 334, 2, 11]; see also Henry WORDER

WATERS (or WARTERS?), Thomas, prisoner of the rebels [319, 331, 334, 2, 11, 30, 37]; [declared] deserter 16 Jun 1783 [51]; see also WORTERS

WATHAM, (or WATHAN, WATHEN), Thomas, prisoner of the rebels [316, 327, 339, 6, 18, 27, 31]

WATHAN, James, discharged 15 Mar 1781 [320, 330, 3]

WATSON, William, prisoner of the rebels [281]

WELCH, Thomas, prisoner of the rebels 19 Jan 1781 [336, 8, 16, 24, 42]

WELTON, James, deserted 7 Aug 1780? or 1782 [315, 333]

WELTON, John, deserted 7 Aug 1780 [332]

WEST, Samuel, deserted 14 Jun 1779 [310]

WHEELER, Isaac, discharged 5 Aug 1782 [36]

WHITE, James, deserted 3 May 1778 [288, 295]; returned & discharged 6 Nov 1778 [295]

WHITE, Samuel, prisoner of the rebels [317, 325, 341, 9, 13, 26, 33]

WHITEWOOD, Thomas, deserted 29 Jun 1779? [327]; deserted 23 Jun 1780 [316]

WILDAW, Richard, discharged 21 Jun 1783 [50]; possibly German

WILDING, Robert, deserted 24 Nov 1775 [255]

WILLIAMS, George, deserted 4 Aug 1782 [36]

WILLIAMS, John, deserted 14 Jul 1782 [36]; discharged 25 Dec 1782 [40, 52]

WILLIAMS, William, Senior, deserted 29 Mar 1781 [315, 332, 333]; might be two persons as only one entry lists as Senior

WILLICKS, David, discharged 2 Dec 1778 [304]

WILLSON, Roger, discharged 24 Dec 1782 [46]

WILSON, John, corporal, prisoner of the rebels [337, 10, 15, 22, 35]

WOOD, Thomas, adjutant, prisoner on parole [315, 333, 39]

WOODCOCK, Samuel, prisoner of the rebels [321, 324, 338, 4, 28, 38]

WOODS, John, deserted 20 Feb 1780 [329]; deserted 23 Jul 1780 [318]; deserted 23 Feb 1782? [323]

WOOLRYCH, Humphrey, discharged 5 Aug 1782 [36]

WOOTON, John, corporal, prisoner of the rebels [40]

WORDER, Henry, prisoner of the rebels [331, 30, 37]; see also Henry WARDER

WORTERS, Thomas, prisoner [331]; see also WATERS

YOUENS (or YOUINGS, YOWENS), Richard, sergeant, prisoner of the rebels [339, 6, 18, 27, 31]

YOUNG, John, deserted 24 Jul 1779 [312]

YOWENS, Richard. See Richard YOUENS

DESERTIONS BY DATE

As previously hypothesized, comparison of places and dates on muster rolls with the dates of desertion might lead to prognoses as to the region in which a deserter might be found in post-war documents (such as the 1790 federal censuses), because the deserters usually fled only relatively short distances from their former regimental cantonments. Furthermore, soldiers who deserted together might be expected to have settled near each other in the American colonies, thus making their identification more certain in later documentation. Hereinafter follows a list of the deserters by date of desertion:

1775 Nov 15 James White

    Nov 23 Philip Gregory

    Nov 24 John Blaker, Robert Wilding

    Nov 25 James Marples

    Nov 27 John Andrews, Thomas Bunting, William Marchant

    Dec 11 Benjamin Mee

    Dec 13 Richard Smith

    Dec 24 Thomas Blunden

1776 Jan 04 Richard Brown

    Jan 25 Thomas Croper

    Jan 26 John Harding, James Nelson

    Jan 27 Noah Cross

    Feb 04 Joseph Hall

    Feb 18 Joseph Biggs

    Mar 10 John Flower

    Mar 20 William Dutten, Samuel Mills

    Mar 25 Thomas Jones, Thomas Timmis (returned)

    Apr 05 Thomas Blasdel

    Apr 06 William Snodgrass, Henry Underhill

    Apr 07 James Murdoch

    Apr 20 John Boskett

    May 01 Alexander Forrest, Thomas Gahe? (Gate?), William Langham

    Jul 12 John Stuart

    Aug 26 William Stone

    Oct 06 James Kelley

    Nov 03 Richard Hull

Nov 17 David Davis

Dec 01 Richard Rollings, William Sergeant

Dec 04 William Medlam

Dec 10 William Pain, Senior

Dec 24 Zachariah Low

1777 Jan 08 Thomas Brown

Jan 21 James Day, Josiah Dugmore, Isaac Pearce, Paul Price, Thomas Richardson, William Ruston, Adam Tilford

Feb 06 Timothy Griffin

Mar 23 James Smith

Mar 24 Daniel Savage

Apr 22 Thomas Clarke, John Vincent

May 03 James White

Jun 19 Patrick Gallaiher

Jun 21 John Brown

Jul 04 Francis Mitchell

Sep 27 James Star

Oct 10 Thomas Bowel, Joseph Brooks, William Jones

Oct 11 John Hamilton, William Harris

Oct 14 William Terral

Oct 23 John Whitfield

Dec 05 Dennis Shelton

1779 Apr 04 Michael Cannon

Apr 06 Jeremiah Mulvey

Apr 12 John Rogers

Apr 28 Thomas Robertson

Apr 29 James Manuell

May 05 John Addair

May 31 Joseph Charles

Jun 09 George Hill, Joseph Horner

Jun 14 Samuel West

Jun 24 William McIntosh

Jun 25 Timothy Griffin

Jun 29 Thomas Whitewood

Jul 05 Josiah Barrow (Burrow?), James Chase, John Ryans

Jul 14 Thomas Hawkens

Jul 24 John Young

1780 Feb 13 Francis Mitchell

Feb 20 Edward Green, John Woods

Mar 02 James Grimes

Apr 06 Jeremiah Mulvey

Apr 12 John Rogers

Apr 28 Thomas Robertson

Apr 29 James Manntle

May 05 John Addair

May 31 Thomas Morris

Jun 16 William Hynes

Jun 23 Thomas Whitewood

Jul 23 John Woods

Aug 07 John Welton

Aug 08 James Welton

Sep 24 David Morris

Oct 10 William Fitzgarrold

Oct 16 William Fitzgarrold

Dec 23 William Baker

1881 Mar 29 William Williams, William Williams, Sr.

Sep 09 James Reed, John Reed

Sep 19 Edward Cook

Nov 13 Samuel Moor

Nov 16 Isaac Burton

Dec 25 William Holden

1882 Feb 23 John Woods

Mar 16 Timothy Renolds

Apr 12 Christopher Hargrove

May 16 Samuel Hooper, John McDonaugh, Timothy Renolds

May 31 Thomas Morris

Jun 05 William Richards

Jul 14 John Williams

Jul 19 John Nealy

Aug 04 George Williams

Aug 07 James Welton

Sep 05   Thomas Morris

Oct 02   Johnson Hughes

Oct 10   William Fitzgerald

1783 May 30   George Eastham, John Gordon

Jun 11   Robert Davis

Jun 16   William Ashby, Edward Atkins, John Avott, Robert Bell, William Bibb, James Bilton, Nicholas Burt, James Burton, Richard Clemmens, William Cook, John Copeland, Thomas Croft, James Crowley, Edward Eagle, Charles Edmonds, John Endell, Tobias Fallard, Peter Filing, John Gardner, Thomas Garey, Andrew Garratt, William Hart, John Janes, Richard Jones, William Lacke, John Lander, Richard Lattermore, Thomas Law, William Law, William Leech, James Lester, Robert Mansfield, John Mayers, Donald McDonald, Lacky McKiver, John Mealing, John Morris, John Owen, William Paine, William Perryman, John Pike, Joseph Priestt, Robert Ryrie, Richard Slater, Richard Stanistreet, John Stevens, John Stevenson, Charles Talbot, Hugh Ternan, John Thompson, James Trickett, Robert Turner, Thomas Waters

---

1. Published previously, in abbreviated form, as "Deserters, Dischargees, and Prisoners of War from the British Seventh Regiment of Foot (Fusiliers) During the American Revolution," National Genealogical Society Quarterly, volume 67 (1979), number 4, pages 255-263.

INDEX

ACHESON, Thomas, 6
ADAMS, John, 9
ADDAIR, John, 9, 18
ALBISON, John, 9
ALEXANDER, John, 2
ALEXANDER, Thomas, 6
ALLEN, Thomas, 6, 9
ANDERSON, William, 2
ANDREW(S), Alexander, 2
ANDREWS, John, 9, 17
ANDREWS, Peter, 2
ARBIGE, John, 9
ARNOLD, George, 9
ASHBY, William, 9, 19
ATKINS, Edward, 9, 19
ATTAWAY, Thomas, 9
AUTHAWAY, Thomas, 9
AVERY, Thomas, 9
AVOTT, John, 9, 19
BAILESS, William, 2
BAILLIE, Edward, 9
BAKER, William, 9, 18

BANNER, John, 9
BARKER, Jonathan, 9
BARKER, William, 6
BARROW, Josiah, 9, 18
BARTHOLOMEW, Robert, 9
BARTHOLOMEW, Thomas, 9
BATTLE, James, 9
BATTLE, John, 9
BAUMER, John, 6
BAXTER, Edward, 6
BAXTER, George, 6
BECHTMAN, John, 4f
BECTMAN, John, 2
BELL, Richard, 9
BELL, Robert, 9, 19
BELTON, James, 9
BENDALL, Nicholas, 9
BENHARD, George, 6
BENNICK, Christopher, 2
BENTLEY, Peter, 2
BERGMEIER, Daniel, 6
BERGMYER, Daniel, 6
BIBB, William, 9, 19
BIGGS, Joseph, 9, 17

BILLON, James, 9
BILTON, James, 9, 19
BINDLER, Antony, 2
BLACKLOCK, John, 9
BLASDEL(L), Thomas, 9, 1
BLUNDEN, Thomas, 10, 17
BONEY, Thomas, 2
BONNER, John, 10
BOSKETT, John, 10, 17
BOUCH, James, 10
BOWEL, Thomas, 10, 18
BOWERS, William, 10
BOY, Joseph, 10
BOYLE, Henry, 6
BRAUNMILLER, Ludwig, 4f
BRAUNMUELLER, Ludwig, 4f
BREMER, Christian, 6
BRIGGS, George, 6
BRINDLEY, James, 2
BRITTAIN, William, 10
BROADERICK, Daniel, 2
BROADHEAD, Samuel, 2
BROOKS, George, 6
BROOKS, Joseph, 10, 18

BROUGHTON, John, 10
BROWN, John, 10, 18
BROWN, Richard, 10, 17
BROWN, Thomas, 10, 18
BROWN, William, 10
BROWN, Zachariah, 6
BROWNE, William, 6
BROWNMILLER, Ludwick, 2
BROWNMULLIER, Ludwick, 2
BRUMBY, James, 2
BRUMBY, Thomas, 2
BUGG, John, 10
BULL, George, 6
BUNGY, Joshua, 10
BUNTING, Thomas, 10, 17
BURK, Ulick, 10
BURN, Richard, 2
BURR, John, 10
BURROW(S), John, 2
BURROW, Josiah, 10, 18
BURT, Nicholas, 10, 19
BURTON, Duke (or Marmaduke), 2
BURTON, Isaac, 10, 18
BURTON, James, 10, 19

CALDWELL, Henry, 10
CALLOW, Thomas, 10
CAMPION, John, 10
CANNON, Michael, 10, 18
CARDER, Isaac, 10
CARMACK, Peter, 10
CARR, John, 10
CARR, William, 10
CARTER, George, 10
CAVE, John, 10
CHACE, James, 10
CHALLINER, George, 10
CHANDLER, George, 10
CHANNILER, George, 10
CHARLES, Joseph, 10, 18
CHASE, James, 10, 18
CHESTERFIELD, William, 2
CLARKE, B. R., 10
CLARKE, Thomas, 10, 18
CLAYTON, Robert, 10
CLEMENS, Richard, 10
CLEMENTS, James, 6
CLEMENTS, Richard, 10
CLEMMENS, Richard, 10, 19
CLUFF, John, 10
COLEMAN, John, 2
COLTON, Henry, 2
COOK, Edward, 10, 18
COOK, Peter, 2
COOK, William, 10, 19
COOPER, Edward, 10
COOPLAND, John, 10
COPELAND, John, 10, 19
COSCOMB, Thomas, 10
COTTON, Henry, 2
COYLE(S), Thomas, 10
CRAFT, Thomas, 10

CRAWFORD, Robert, 2
CROFT, Thomas, 10, 19
CROPER, Thomas, 10, 17
CROSS, Noahn, 10, 17
CROW, Charles, 10
CROWLEY, Cornelius, 10
CROWLEY, James, 10, 19
CUBELAR, John, 6
CURTICE, Edward, 10
CURTICE, Richard, 10
CURTIS, Edward, 10
CUSHNER, Alexander, 10
DABNEY, William, 11
DANDY, John, 11
DAVIDSON, Jonathan, 6
DAVIES, William, 6
DAVIS, Benjamin, 11
DAVIS, David, 11, 18
DAVIS, Robert, 11, 19
DAVIS, Thomas, 11
DAVIS, William, 6
DAWSON, Thomas, 11
DAY, James, 11, 18
DEPRARD, John, 11
DESPARD, John, 11
DEVELYN, Arthur, 2
DICKENS, John, 11
DICKINGS, John, 11
DICKINS, John, 11
DINGLEY, Thomas, 11
DOOZLEY, Samuel, 2
DORSON, Thomas, 11
DOWLING, Jeremiah, 11
DOWNEY, William, 11
DOYAL, James, 2
DUDDEN, William, 11
DUGMORE, Josiah, 11, 18

DUNN, Andrew, 2
DUNN, Carroll, 6
DUNN, Thomas, 11
DUTTEN, William, 11, 17
EAGLE, Edward, 11, 19
EAMES, Robert, 2
EASTHAM, George, 11, 19
EATON, George, 11
EDMONDS, Charles, 11, 19
EDMONDS, John, 6
EDMONDS, Thomas, 6
EDWARDS, John, 11
EGGLETON, Thomas, 2
ENDELL, John, 11, 19
ENDLE, John, 11
ERHART, Frederick, 6
ERHART, John, 6
ETZELL, John, 6
EVELEIGH, William, 11
EWER, William, 11
EWRE, William, 11
FAITHFULL, William, 2
FALL, Francis, 2
FALLARD, Tobias, 11, 19
FAMDEN, John, 2
FENIMORE, Humphrey, 2
FILING, Peter, 11, 19
FILLING, Peter, 11
FISCHBACH, Toennis, 4f
FISHBACK, Dennis, 2
FISHBACK, Francis, 11
FITZGARROLD, William, 11, 18
FITZGERALD, William, 11, 19
FLEMMING, Andrew, 2
FLOWER, John, 11, 17
FLOYD, John, 6
FLUCK, William, 11

FOLLARD, Tobias, 11
FORBES, Henry, 11
FORREST, Alexander, 11, 17
FOX, James, 11
FOX, Thomas, 11
FOYLINGS, Peter, 11
FRANKLIN, William, 6
FRAZER, James, 2
FREEMAN, William, 11
FRICKETT, Joseph, 11
FRISKIN, George, 11
FULLARD, Tobias, 11
FYLING, Peter, 11
GAHE, Thomas, 11, 17
GAILLAIHER, Patrick, 11, 18
GARDENER, John, 11
GARDINER, John, 2, 11
GARDNER, John, 11, 19
GAREY, Thomas, 11, 19
GARRATT, Andrew, 11, 19
GARRATT, William, 11
GARY, Thomas, 11
GASCOMB, Thomas, 11
GATE, Thomas, 11, 17
GENTLE, Edward, 11
GEORGE, Jacob, 6
GILES, William, 11
GIL(L)MAN, Francis, 11
GLOVER, Richard, 11
GOOD, Arthur, 2
GORDON, John, 12, 19
GOSCOMB, Thomas, 12
GRACE, Thomas, 12
GRACE, William, 12
GRAY, James, 12
GRAY, Thomas, 12

GREEN, Clem, 12
GREEN, Daniel, 12
GREEN, Dennis, 6
GREEN, Edward, 12, 18
GREEN, Samuel, 12
GREEN, William, 6
GREGORY, Philip, 12, 17
GRIFFIN, John, 12
GRIFFIN, Timothy, 12, 18
GRIMES, James, 12, 18
GRISSEN, Clem, 12
GROCE, William, 12
GROW, William, 12
GUYE, Thomas, 2
HALL, Joseph, 17
HALL, Thomas, 12
HAMILTON, James, 2
HAMILTON, John, 18
HAMILTON, William, 2
HARBIGE, John, 12
HARBRIDGE, John, 12
HARBRIGE, John, 12
HARDING, John, 12, 17
HARDY, George, 12
HARGROVE, Christopher, 12, 18
HARKINS, Charles, 6
HARNOTT, John, 2
HARRIS, Francis, 6
HARRIS, John, 12
HARRIS, William, 12, 18
HARRISON, John, 12
HARRISON, Joseph, 12
HARRISON, Joshua, 12
HARRISON, Josiah, 12
HARRISS, Francis, 6
HARRISS, John, 12

HART, William, 12, 19
HARVEY, William, 12
HATFIELD, John, 2
HAUSEN, John van, 3
HAWKENS, Thomas, 12, 18
HAWORTH, James, 12
HAYS, James, 12
HAZEL, Benjamin, 12
HAZLE, Benjamin, 12
HAZLEHURST, John, 2
HEARD, John, 12
HEARD, William, 12
HEATH, Henry, 12
HEATHERLY, Thomas, 2
HEAZEL, Benjamin, 12
HEBERY, John, 12
HEFLING, George, 6
HENLY, James, 2
HERBERT, William, 2
HIBERY, John, 12
HICKEY, Thomas, 6
HICKS, Thomas, 12
HIGGINS, Thomas, 6
HILL, George, 12, 18
HILL, John, 2
HILL, Richard, 6
HILL, Thomas, 12
HILSON, John, 12
HILTON, John, 12
HOBBINGS, Jacob, 2
HOCHMEIER, George, 6
HODGES, Thomas, 12
HOEFLING, George, 6
HOGAN, Michael, 12
HOHMEIER, George, 6
HOLDEN, John, 2

HOLDEN, William, 12, 18
HOLLAND, John, 2
HOLLOWAY, Thomas, 12
HOLTSMAN, Michael, 6
HOLTZMANN, Michael, 6
HOMYER, George, 6
HOOKER, Henry, 12
HOOPER, Samuel, 12, 18
HORNER, Joseph, 12, 18
HORTON, George, 12
HOWARTH, George, 12
HOWARTH, James, 12
HOWORTH, James, 12
HOYD, John, 6
HOYDE, John, 6
HUBERT, Michael, 6
HUDSON, John, 12
HUGHES, Charles, 12
HUGHES, John, 12
HUGHES, Johnson, 12, 19
HUGHS, Andrew, 2
HUGHS, Charles, 12
HULL, Richard, 13, 17
HUNT, Edmund, 13
HUSBAND(S), Charles, 13
HYNES, William, 13, 18
INGRAM, Henry, 13
IRWIN, Christopher, 13
JAMES, John, 6
JAMISON, Joseph, 2
JANES, John, 13, 19
JANNERY, John, 13
JARMAN, Daniel, 2
JARRATT, Andrew, 13
JEACH, William, 13
JEAN(E)S, John, 13

JEFFERY, Robert, 13
JEMMISON, Joseph, 2
JENKINS, John, 13
JOHNSON, Joseph, 13
JONES, James, 13
JONES, John, 13
JONES, Joseph, 6
JONES, Richard, 13, 19
JONES, Robert, 2
JONES, Thomas, 13, 17
JONES, William, 13, 18
KAVENAUGH, Thomas, 2
KELLEY, Daniel, 13
KELLEY, James, 13, 17
KELLY, Daniel, 13
KENADEY, John, 6
KENNADY, Nathaniel, 2
KENNEDY, William, 13
KEY, John, 2
KIETH, James, 6
KIRBY, Thomas, 13
KIRSCHNER, Alexander, 13
KIRS(C)HNER, Philip, 6
KNIEBEL, Christian, 6
KNOEBEL, Christian, 6
KNOWLES, James, 13
KNOWLES, Joshua, 13
KUEBLER, John, 6
KYRIE, Robert, 13
LACKE, William, 13, 19
LAMBOURN, Thomas, 13
LANDER, John, 13, 19
LANGFORD, John, 13
LANGFORD, Thomas, 2
LANGHAM, William, 13, 17
LATTAMORE, Richard, 13

LATTERMORE, Richard, 13, 19
LATTIMORE, Richard, 13
LAVENDER, William, 13
LAVORY, Richard, 13
LAW, Thomas, 13, 19
LAW, William, 19
LAWRENCE, Alfred, 13
LAWRENCE, William, 2
LEACH, William, 13
LE(E)BECK, Anthony, 6
LEECH, William, 19
LEEDS, John, 13
LEEMAN, Diedrick, 6
LEGFORD, John, 6
LEHMANN, Diedrick, 6
LEISTER, James, 13
LENAN, Thomas, 13
LENNON, Thomas, 13
LENON, Thomas, 13
LESTER, James, 13, 19
LESTER, Robert, 13
LIDDLE, Thomas, 13
LINE, Thomas, 6
LING, George, 3
LITTLEWOOD, Thomas, 13
LOCK, William, 13
LOCKE, William, 13
LODDY, James, 13
LOMAX, John, 13
LOMAX, Marsn?, 13
LONG, William, 13
LORANCE, William, 2
LOVATT, Lovat, 13
LOW, William, 13
LOW, Zachariah, 13, 18
LOWE, Samuel, 3
LUCAS, William, 13
LUEBECK, Anthony, 6
LUMPIE, Anthony, 3
LYTCH, John Peter, 3
MABBERLY, Joseph, 3
MAGEE, George, 6
MANEY, William, 3
MANNTLE, James, 13, 18
MANSFIELD, Robert, 13, 19
MANUELL, James, 14, 18
MARCHANT, William, 14, 17
MARLOW, Samuel, 3
MARPLES, James, 14, 17
MARRICK(S), John, 14
MARSH, James, 3
MARSHMAN, Jeremiah, 6
MASLIN, Robert, 6
MATHEWS, William, 14
MATTHEWS, James, 3
MATTHEWS, William, 14
MAYCOCK, Thomas, 14
MAYERS, John, 14, 19
MAZIE, John, 14
McCLOUD, Alexander, 14
McCOLLUM, John, 6
McDONALD, Angus, 3
McDONALD, Donald, 14, 19
McDONALD, James, 14
McDONAUGH, John, 14, 18
McGEE, James, 3
McHARRY, James, 3
McHIVER, Lacky, 14
McINTOSH, William 14, 18
McKELLER, Dougal, 3
McKENZIE, James, 6
McKINZIE, Valentin, 3
McKIVER, Lacky, 14, 19
McLEOD, Alexander, 14
McLEOD, Donald, 14
McMAHAN, --, 6
McVEAGH, Edward, 13
McVICKERS, Daniel, 14
MEALING, John, 14, 19
MEALING, Richard, 14
MEANS, John, 14
MEARS, John, 14
MEASEY, John, 14
MEDLAM, William, 14, 18
MEE, Benjamin, 14, 17
MERAR, William, 14
MERCER, William, 14
MEREDITH, David, 6
MERRICK, John, 14
MEYRICK, John, 14
MIDDLEWOOD, Robert, 3
MILES, Thomas, 14
MILLER, James, 6
MILLER, John, 14
MILLIGAN, George, 7
MILLS, Samuel, 14, 17
MITCHELL, Francis, 14, 18
MOHRANZ, Conrad, 4f
MOON, Samuel, 14
MOOR, Samuel, 14, 18
MOORE, George, 7
MORREANCE, Conrade, 3
MORRIS, David, 14, 18
MORRIS, John, 14, 19
MORRIS, Thomas, 14, 18, 19
MORSANCE, Conrade, 3
MORTON, John, 14
MORTON, William, 14
MOSELEY, John, 7
MOSELY, George, 7
MOSEY, John, 14
MOSS, Joseph, 3
MULLEN, Brian, 3
MULVEY, Jeremiah, 14, 18
MUMFORD, Stephen, 14
MURDOCH, James, 14, 17
MURPHY, James, 14
MUZIE, John, 14
NEABLE, Christian, 7
NEALING, James, 3
NEALING, Richard, 14
NEALY, John, 14, 18
NELLEY, John, 14
NELSON, James, 14, 17
NEWELL, Henry, 14
NEWEY, Thomas, 14
NEWTON, James, 14
NEWY, Thomas, 14
NICHOLS, James, 14
NIEBEL, Christian, 7
NORMAN, James, 14
OAKES, Thomas, 3
ODELL, John, 14
ORD, George, 3
OSBORNE, William, 7
OWEN, John, 14, 19
PAIN, William, Senior, 15, 18
PAINE, William, 15, 19
PARKER, John, 15
PARKES, 15
PARKINSON, John, 15
PARVIS, Ben, 3
PATTISON, George, 7
PEARCE, Isaac, 15, 18
PEET, John, 3

PERCIVALL, Frances, 15
PERRY, Benjamin, 7
PERRYMAN, William, 15, 19
PETERS, Joseph, 15
PFEILING, Peter, 15
PFEULING, Peter, 15
PHILLIPS, William, 15
PIKE, John, 15, 19
PLAW, John, 15
PLUCKNETT, John, 7
PLUNKETT, Abraham, 7
POWEL, William, 15
POWER, William, 7
PRICE, John, 15
PRICE, Paul, 15, 18
PRICE, Richard, 15
PRIEST(T), Joseph, 15
PRIEST, Robert, 15
QUIN, Thomas, 3
RATHBONE, Benjamin, 15
REED, James, 15, 18
REED, John, 15, 18
REED, William, 3
REEVES, William, 7
RENOLDS, Timothy, 15, 18
REYNOLDS, James, 15
REYNOLDS, Timothy, 15
RICHARDS, William, 15, 18
RICHARDSON, Thomas, 15, 18
RICHMOND, James, 7
RICKETTS, Joseph, 15
RIELY, Patrick, 3
RIGGS, William, 7
RIGLEY, William, 15
RIRIE, Robert, 15
RIVETT, James, 3

ROBERTSON, Thomas, 15, 18
ROGERS, John, 15, 18
ROGERS, Peter, 15
ROLLINGS, Richard, 15, 18
ROSE, Robert, 7
ROSS, David, 7
ROWLAND, Edward, 15
ROWLAND, John, 15
RUSTON, William, 15, 18
RYAN, John, 15
RYANS, John, 18
RYDER, Thomas, 15
RYLEY, Matthew, 15
RYRIE, ROBERT, 15, 19
SANBIDGE, Thomas, 15
SAVAGE, Daniel, 15, 18
SAVORY, Richard, 15
SCHEINEMANN, Frederick, 7
SCHLEICHEN, Peter, 4f
SCHWAR(T)Z, Leonhard, 4f
SEBERT, Henry, 3
SEEDS, James, 3
SENNETT, Patrick, 15
SENNITT, Patrick, 15
SERGEANT, William, 15, 18
SHARP, John, 15
SHAUGHNESSY, Michael, 7
SHELTON, Dennis, 18
SHELTON, John, 15
SHERIDEN, John, 7
SHIBLIE, John, 3
SHINYMAN, Frederick, 7
SHIPLEY, John, 3
SHLYGEN, Peter, 3
SHORT, Thomas, 15
SHORTO, Thomas, 15

SHORTTOE, Thomas, 15
SIBLEY, John, 15
SIBLIE, John, 15
SILLS, William, 3
SILVIE, Benjamin, 3
SLATER, George, 15
SLATER, James, 15
SLATER, John, 15
SLATER, Michael, 15
SLATER, Richard, 15, 19
SMALLWOOD, William, 15
SMITH, Daniel, 15
SMITH, Francis, 3
SMITH, James, 15, 18
SMITH, John, 15
SMITH, Nathan, 3
SMITH, Richard, 16, 17
SMITH, Samuel, 3
SMITH, Thomas, 7
SNODGRASS, William, 16, 17
SPEAKER, John, 3
SPENCER, Thomas, 7, 16
SPENDLER, Anthony, 3
SPERWOOD, Timothy, 6
SPYCER, Francis, 16
SPYER, Francis, 16
STAHL, John, 7
STALL, John, 7
STANIS(S)TREET, Richard, 16, 19
STANLEY, Michael, 16
STANNESSTREET, Richard, 16
STAR, James, 16, 18
STAYDON, William, 3
STEVENS, Alexander, 16
STEVENS, John, 7, 16, 19

STEVENSON, John, 16, 19
STEVENSON, Thomas, 16
STEWART, Alexander, 16
STOLLARD, Robert, 3
STONE, William, 16, 17
STORCH, William, 7
STORKE, William, 7
STOVER, William, 16
STRACHAN, John, 3
STROUD, John, 3
STUART, Alexander, 7, 16
STUART, John, 16, 17
SUCH, William, 17
SUFFOLK, George, 16
SULLIVAN, Daniel, 7
SULLIVAN, John, 7
SUNDERLAND, John, 16
SUTHERLAND, Daniel, 16
SWARTS, Leonard, 3
SWENY, Francis, 7
SYMONDS, Ephraim, 16
TAFT, Thomas, 3
TALBOT(T), Charles, 16, 19
TAMFREY, William, 3
TAYLOR, Dimock, 7
TAYLOR, Simon, 7
TAYLOR, Thomas, 7
TAYSON, Timothy, 16
TERNAN, Hugh, 16, 19
TERNON, Hugh, 16
TERRAL, William, 16, 18
THIFRIES, Frederick, 3
THOMAS, John, 16
THOMPSON, John, 3, 16, 19
THOMSON, John, 3
THORNHILL, Peter, 16

THORNTON, George, 16
TIBBISH, Francis, 16
TIBBISH, Imanuel, 16
TILFORD, Adam, 16, 18
TILLEY, Robert, 7
TIMINSON, Joseph, 3
TIMMIS, Thomas, 16, 17
TINKLER, William, 16
TINKLEY, William, 16
TINNERY, John, 16
TOMINSON, Joseph, 3
TONG(UE), William, 16
TOWERS. Dennis, 16
TRACEY, James, 3
TRICKETT, James, 16, 19
TRICKETT(S), Joseph, 16
TUCKER, Thomas, 16
TURNER, Robert, 16, 19
UNDERHILL, Henry, 16, 17
VAN HAUSEN, John, 3
VICKERS, John, 16
VINCENT, John, 16, 18
VOWELLS, John, 3
WALKER, William, 16
WALLNE, John, 3
WALSH, William, 7
WARD, George, 16
WARDELL, John, 16
WARDER, Henry, 16
WARRAN, William, 3
WARTERS, Thomas, 16
WATERS, Thomas, 16, 19
WATERS, William, 3
WATHAM, Thomas, 16
WATHAN, James, 16
WATHAN, Thomas, 16
WATHEN, Thomas, 16
WATSON, James, 3
WATSON, William, 17
WATTS, Daniel, 7
WELCH, Thomas, 17
WELTON, James, 17, 18
WELTON, John, 17, 18
WEST, Jonathan, 7
WEST, Richard, 3
WEST, Samuel, 17, 18
WHEELER, Isaac, 17
WHITE, James, 17, 18
WHITE, John, 7
WHITE, Samuel, 17
WHITEWOOD, Thomas, 17, 18
WHITFIELD, John, 18
WHITWHAM, William, 3
WILDAW, Richard, 17
WILDING, Robert, 17
WILLIAMS, George, 17, 18
WILLIAMS, John, 17, 18
WILLIAMS, William, 17, 18
WILLIAMS, William, Sr., 18
WILLICKS, David, 17
WILLSON, Roger, 17
WILSON, John, 17
WILSON, Thomas, 7
WOOD, Thomas, 17
WOODCOCK, Samuel, 17
WOODS, John, 17, 18
WOOLRYCH, Humphrey, 17
WOOTON, John, 17
WORDER, Henry, 17
WORTERS, Thomas, 17
WRANGHAM, George, 3
YOUENS, Richard, 17
YOUINGS, Richard, 17
YOUNG, John, 17, 18
YOWENS, Richard, 17

British-American Genealogical Research
Monograph Number 9, Part 2

BRITISH AND GERMAN DESERTERS, DIS- CHARGEES, AND PRISONERS OF WAR WHO MAY HAVE REMAINED IN CANADA AND THE UNITED STATES, 1774-1783: Part 2

Clifford Neal Smith

First Printing, November 1989   UZ

Introduction

A general introduction to this study will be found in Part One of this monograph.

***

DESERTERS, DISCHARGEES, AND PRISONERS OF WAR FROM THE BRITISH TENTH REGIMENT OF FOOT (NORTH LINCOLNSHIRE)[1]

The muster rolls for the Tenth Regiment of Foot are to be found in the Public Records Office, London, in W.O. 12, volume 2750. The following list of names has been gleaned from seventeen muster rolls therein, as follows:

```
A--Boston, 19 Jan 1775
B--Boston, 29 Sep 1775
C--Boston, 02 Feb 1776?
D--Boston, 02 Feb 1776
E--Staten Island, 12 Jul 1776
F--Staten Island, 17 May 1777
G--Brunswick [New Jersey], 22 Apr 1777
H--Staten Island, 18 May 1777
I--Brunswick, 19 Apr 1777
J--Philadelphia, 28 Mar 1778
K--Philadelphia, 06 Feb 1778
L--Philadelphia, 23 Feb 1778
M--Staten Island, 21 Sep 1778
N--Richmond [Staten Island], 21 Sep 1778
O--Berwick upon Tweed [England], 26 Mar 1779
P--Staten Island, 21 Jul 1778
Q--Richmond [Staten Island], 2 Jul 1778
```

The list is probably incomplete, because this writer abstracted only names appearing on muster rolls beginning in 1774, without realizing that the Regiment had been stationed in Boston since 1768. Consequently, deserters and dischargees during the period 1768-1774 are not listed herein.

The Tenth Regiment was stationed in Ireland during the whole of the Seven Years' War, known in America as the French and Indian War. When the disputes between Great Britain and her North American colonies began to assume a serious aspect, the Tenth was one of the first corps ordered to proceed across the Atlantic. The regiment embarked from Ireland in the spring of 1767, and after a short stay in Nova Scotia, was ordered to Boston, "where, in 1768, the conduct of the populace assumed so violent a character as to render the presence of a military force necessary." The historical record discloses no particular activity for the Regiment on garrison duty in Boston until 1775. From that year until it was returned to England in 1778, however, the Regiment was actively engaged in campaigns against the rebels. Because knowledge of the movements of the unit during that period is important in predicting the place of desertion or imprisonment, the following outline will be useful to genealogical researchers:

1775 In April flank companies of the Regiment advanced on Concord and Lexington. After the foray, these companies returned to Boston, having suffered some casualties.

1776 In March the Tenth Regiment removed to Halifax, Nova Scotia, where it remained until June, when it sailed for Staten Island, arriving in early July. Here, reinforcements were received from England.

In late August the Tenth landed on Long Island, took Brooklyn, and then crossed to New York Island (Manhattan).

In October the Regiment proceeded up the river to West Chester (now Westchester), where it went ashore. Reembarking, it sailed for Pell's Point and forced the Americans to abandon fortifications at White Plains.

In November the Tenth participated in the siege of Fort Washington and Fort Lee with minor losses.

In December the Regiment was detached to sail against Rhode Island, which was quickly reduced.

1777 In June the troops reembarked for New Jersey.

In August the Regiment again took ship and sailed to Chesapeake Bay, proceeding up the Elk River and landing at Elk Ferry.

In September the Regiment participated in the offensive against the Americans at Chad's Ford, passing on to Concord, Ashtown, and on the 25th camped in Germantown.

On 29 September the Tenth was detached from the camp at Germantown and ordered to attack a strong American redoubt at Billing's Point on the Jersey shore of the Delaware River across from Chester.

In the middle of October the British Army, including the Tenth Regiment, entered Philadelphia, where it set up permanent quarters.

In December the Tenth was sent to attack an enemy camp at Whitemarsh, but returned without success.

1778 The entry of France into the war on the side of the American rebels so completely changed the nature of the war that the British decided to evacuate Philadelphia and return to New York.

In June the British army marched overland through New Jersey, encountering minor harassment until reaching Freehold, where sharp fighting took place, with some casualties to the Tenth Regiment. The army continued northward to Sandy Hook and embarked for New York. "The Tenth had lost many men during the period they had been in America, from fatigue, privation, disease, and other casualties, besides those killed and disabled in action, ... and soon after the Regiment arrived at New York, it was selected to return to England. The men fit for service, who volunteered to remain in the country, were transferred to other corps, and the remainder embarked from New York towards the end of October; they arrived in England in December."[2]

A recapitulation of the 37 soldiers known to have deserted from the Tenth Regiment shows that eleven men deserted while the Regiment was stationed at Boston (1774-1775), one man at Halifax (1776), seven men in Rhode Island (1777), sixteen men at Philadelphia and environs (1777-1778), and two men in New Jersey or at New York (1778). Normally, desertions tended to peak shortly before embarkation for England, and it is suspected that a number of the men transferred to other regiments may have deserted shortly after October 1778. (The reports of their desertion probably are shown in muster rolls of regiments to which they were reassigned.)

Surnames preceded by an asterisk are probably German. There were many German recruits in the regular British army at the time.

ALLEN, Jonathan, p.o.w. (E:165; H:171; J:186, 194; O:207; Q:221)

ALLEN, Richard, discharged 24 May 1777 (J:184)

ANNALY, Luke, deserted 15 Jan 1775 (B:144)

ANSON, John, prisoner of war (J:186, 194; Q:221)

ANTWISTLE, Arthur, discharged 24 May 1777 (J:183)

ASHWORTH (ASKWORTH; ASWORTH), Samuel, prisoner of war (J:186, 194; O:207; Q:221)

ATKINS, William, discharged 24 Aug 1776 (F:175)

BALL, Charles, prisoner of war (J:179, 189; M:202; O:212; P:224)

BAMFIELD (BARNFIELD), James, prisoner of war (J:187; O:214; P:215)

BARNETT, William, prisoner of war (J:178, 188)

BELK (BILK), Jonathan, prisoner of war (J:183, 193; P:218)

BENNET, Robert, prisoner of war (M:201)

*BERGER, John, prisoner of war (J:186, 194; O:207; Q:221)

*BEYER, John, deserted 26 Jun 1777 (J:184, 191)

BILK. See BELK

BONER (BONNER), Hugh, prisoner of war (J:179, 189; M:202; P:224)

BOYD, Hugh, discharged 29 Feb 1777 (J:178)

BOYD, William, discharged 24 Dec 1775 (D:152)

BRADSHAW, John, prisoner of war (J:177, 187)

BRIEN, Stephen, prisoner of war (D:149)

CAMPLE [CAMPBELL?], Daniel, prisoner of war (J:194)

*CANITZ (CONITZ), Sebastian, Corporal, deserted 26 Feb 1778 (J:178, 188; P:216)

CANNON, George, discharged 29 Apr 1775 (B:138)

CARELTON, John, prisoner of war (O:211)

CARELTON. See also CHARELTON

CARSON, Samuel, discharged 22 May 1777 (J:180)

CASEY. See KEACY

CHAMBERS, John, prisoner of war (O:211)

CHAMBERS, Richard, prisoner of war (J:180, 190; P:217; Q:225)

CHARELTON (CHARLETON, CHARLTON), Thomas, prisoner of war (J:180, 190; P:217; Q:225)

CHARELTON. See also CARELTON

CLAIN. See KLANE

CLARK, Thomas, deserted 22 Dec 1774 (A:129)

*CLINARD, William, transferred to the Hessians 12 May 1777 (J:178)

COLLINS, William, prisoner of war (D:149; F:169; J:178, 188; N:203; O:213; P:216)

COMMINS, Richard, discharged 25 Sep 1778 (O:206)

CONITZ. See CANITZ

CONNERS, Moses, discharged 24 Apr 1777 (J:177, 187; P:215)

COOK, William, prisoner of war (J:194; Q:221)

COOPER, Francis, discharged 24 Aug 1777 (J:189)

COOPER, Grant, discharged 24 Aug 1777 (J:179)

COVENEY (COVENY), John, discharged 24 Apr 1778 (J:178, 188; P:216)

CRISSWELL, James, discharged 24 Apr 1778 (Q:223)

*CRUSE, John, discharged 24 Aug 1776 (H:172)

CURREN (CURRIN), Edward, prisoner of war (J:184, 191; M:201; O:205; P:220)

DAGG, Thomas, Sergeant, discharged 24 Oct 1774 (A:131)

*DAMMON (DAMON), Conrade, prisoner of war (J:186, 194; O:207; Q:221)

DAVIS, John, discharged 25 Jul 1774 (A:133)

DEAN, William, discharged 24 May 1777 (J:186)

*DICKMAN, Henry, deserted 28 May 1778 (P:220)

DOWDS, William, discharged 25 Sep 1778 (O:211)

DUNLAP, John, deserted 8 Oct 1778 (O:206)

DUNMAID, Thomas, discharged 22 May 1777 (J:180)

DUNN, Thomas, prisoner of war (J:183, 193; M:198; O:208; P:218)

ELLIOT (ELLIOTT), Gabez (Jabez), prisoner of war (E:159; F:170; J:179, 189; M:202; O:212; P:224)

ELLIS, Edmond, discharged 24 May 1777 (J:186)

ELLIS, William, deserted 29 Sep 1775 (B:140); deserted 29 Dec 1775 (D:155)

EVANS, John, Sergeant, prisoner of war (J:179, 189; M:202; P:224)

FAIR, William, deserted 8 Oct 1778 (O:208)

FAIRLEY, James, prisoner of war (F:174)

FARMER, William, prisoner of war (J:178, 188; N:203; O:213; P:216)

FORKE (FORKEY), John, prisoner of war (J:180; O:207; P:217)

FOWLER, Robert, prisoner of war (J:179, 189; P:224)

*FRANKS, Peter, Corporal, prisoner of war (J:177, 187; M:204; O:214; P:215)

FRAPWELL, William, deserted 6 Oct 1777 (J:179, 189)

GALPIN. See GULPIN

GARDINER, Thomas, discharged 6 Oct 1775 (C:147)

GARVEY, William, prisoner of war (F:176; J:184, 191; M:201; O:205; P:220)

GEFFERY (JEFFERY), Samuel, prisoner of war (J:180, 190)

GILLROY (GILROY), John, Corporal, prisoner of war (E:164; F:176)

GILPIN. See GULPIN

GLENN (GLINN), John, prisoner of war (J:186, 194; O:207; Q:221)

*GOADBROTH, Ludvick, deserted 17 Jun 1778 (P:217)

GRANT, Peter, discharged 24 Jul 1774 (D:148)

GULPIN, John, discharged 24 Jul 1774 (A:131)

*GUTBROT. See Goadbroth

HAILS (HALES, HALLES), John, prisoner of war (J:180, 190; O:211; P:217; Q:225)

HALDON, William, discharged 24 Aug 1776 (F:167)

HALL, Nebuch[adnezza]r, discharged 24 Apr 1778 (J:188; P:216)

HALLES. See HAILS

*HALSINDINE (HASKINDINE), George, prisoner of war (J:180, 190; P:217)

HALSINDINE. See also HELSENDEGER; HELSENDEGN

HANDS, James, discharged 1 Oct 1774 (A:132)

HANIFORD (HANNIFORD), Ephraim, prisoner of war (M:199; O:2067; P:221)

HANKEY, Richard, Ensign, prisoner of war (J:179, 189)

HARDEN (HARDIN, HARDON), Thomas, prisoner of war (J:180; P:217; Q:225)

HARDEN, William, prisoner of war (O:211)

HASKINDINE. See HALSINDINE; HELSENDEGER; HELSENDEGN

*HEAGUE, Anthony, deserted 21 May 1777 (J:185)

*HEIMPEL. See HIMPLES

*HELSENDEGER, Frederick, prisoner of war (O:211)

*HELSENDEGN, George, prisoner of war (Q:225)

*HELSENDEGN. See also HALSINDINE

HICKEY, Charles, prisoner of war (D:148; E:164; F:176; J:184, 191)

HICKEY, Michael, prisoner of war (O:210; P:219, 226)

*HIMPLES, Christian, deserted 19 Jun 1778 (P:216)

*HIRTH, William, discharged 1 Nov 1774 (A:135)

HOEFER; HOFER. See HUFFER

HOLBROCK (HOLBROOK), John, prisoner of war (J:184, 191; M:201; O:205; P:220)

HOLMES, Benjamin, prisoner of war (J:184, 191; M:201; O:205; P:220)

*HUFFER, Joseph, prisoner of war (J:185, 196; M:197; P:222)

*HUFFER, William, prisoner of war (O:206)

HUGHES, David, discharged 24 Apr 1778 (J:184, 191; P:220)

HUTCHINSON, Charles, deserted 9 Dec 1774 (A:131)

INGRAM, Francis, prisoner of war (J:184, 191; M:201; O:205; P:220)

JACKSON, George, prisoner of war (P:219)

*JAGGAR (JAGGER), Abraham, prisoner of war (O:210; P:219, 226)

JEFFERY. See GEFFERY

JENKINS, Thomas, prisoner of war (F:169)

JUNG. See YOUNG

KANITZ. See CANITZ

KEACY, Robert, deserted 21 Jun 1777 (J:180)

*KELLER, Conrad, deserted 22 May 1778 (P:217)

KELLEY (KELLY), Theodore, prisoner of war (P:217; Q:225)

KELLY, Augustus, prisoner of war (O:211)

KELLY, Thomas, prisoner of war (J:190)

KENADY, Thomas, discharged 6 Oct 1775 (D:155)

KLANE, George, deserted 21 Jun 1777 (J:180)

KONITZ. See CANITZ

LAMPRECHT. See LAMPRIGHT

*LAMPRIGHT, Andrew, prisoner of war (J:179, 189; P:224)

LEE, James, prisoner of war (O:212)

LEE, Samuel, prisoner of war (E:159; F:170; J:189; M:202; P:224), discharged 25 Sep 1778 (O:214)

LEWIS, Thomas, prisoner of war (M:197)

McCASH, Adam, prisoner of war (J:184, 191; M:201; O:205; P:220)

McCONKEY, John, Sergeant, prisoner of war (D:148; E:162; F:174; J:185, 196)

McCREA, John, discharged 6 Oct 1775 (D:153)

McDONALD, Alexander, deserted 29 Sep 1775 (B:140; D:155)

McDONALD, David, Corporal, discharged 24 Apr 1778 (J:191; P:220)

McEUIN, George, discharged 23 Feb 1777 (G:168; J:181)

McGAW, Alexander, prisoner of war (J:183, 193; M:198; O:208; P:218)

McGEE, Charles, discharged 23 Feb 1777 (J:183, 193; P:218)

McGRATH, Gilbert, prisoner of war (J:186, 194; M:199; O:207; P:221)

McGRATH, James discharged 24 Apr 1778 (J:186; Q:221); discharged 24 Sep 1778 (J:194)

McKENZIE, Daniel, Junior, enlisted 24 Oct 1777 (J:194)

McKENZIE, Daniel, Senior, prisoner of war (J:194)

McKENZIE, William, prisoner of war (J:188; P:216)

McLEOD, Mungo, prisoner of war (J:184, 191; M:201; O:205; P:220)

McPHERSON, John, deserted 14 May 1778 (P:220)

MARDON, Thomas, prisoner of war (J:190)

*MARIE, Ludovick, deserted 11 Sep 1777 (J:178, 188)

MARKHAM, Edward, prisoner of war (P:215)

MARLOW, Patrick, discharged 6 Oct 1775 (C:147)

MARSDEN (MAUSDEN), David, prisoner of war (J:194; M:199; O:207; P:221)

MARTAIN, William, prisoner of war (J:184, 191)

MARTIN, James, discharged 25 Sep 1778 (O:210)

MAUSDON. See MARSDEN

MAWHENY, Samuel, discharged 10 Feb 1775 (B:142)

MELLON, Thomas, deserted 2 Jun 1776 (E:164)

MERDYTH, James, discharged 23 Feb 1777 (J:178)

MERIDIETH, John, discharged 24 Dec 1775 (D:152)

MERRITT, Isaac, discharged 24 Aug 1776 (F:167)

MILLEGAN, John, discharged 25 Sep 1778 (O:207)

MITCHELL, Henry, deserted 23 Jun 1777 (K:182)

MOORE, Robert, prisoner of war (J:178, 188; N:203; O:213; P:216)

MORRISON, George, prisoner of war (D:152; E:166; H:172)

MULHALL, Thomas, deserted 6 Oct 1775 (D:151)

MURDOCH (MURDOCK), George, prisoner of war (J:180, 190)

MURRAY, Gregory, prisoner of war (J:183, 193)

NELSON, John, discharged 6 Oct 1775 (D:155)

NOONAN (NOONON), John, prisoner of war (J:179, 189; M:202; O:212; P:224)

NUTT, John, prisoner of war (J:178, 188)

ORMAND (ORMON, ORMOND), James, prisoner of war (J:188; N:203; O:213; P:216)

PARKE, John, prisoner of war (J:190)

PATTERSON, Robert, discharged 24 May 1777 (J:185)

*PICKARD, Frederick, deserted 19 Jun 1778 (P:216)

POTTER, James, prisoner of war (O:210; P:219, 226)

PRATT, John, discharged 25 Sep 1778 (O:206)

*PRETZLOW, Caspar, prisoner of war (O:214)

*PRITCHLER, Caspar, prisoner of war (J:187; M:204; P:215) [probably same man as PRETZLOW]

PURDY, Robert, discharged 24 Apr 1778 (J:186, 194; Q:221)

RAWLINS, Richard, prisoner of war (J:194)

REILY (RIELY, RILEY), Patrick, prisoner of war (J:181; K:192; M:202; O:212; P:224)

*REPKEY (RIPKEY, RIPLEY), Gerard, prisoner of war (F:169; J:178, 188; N:203; P:216)

RICHISON, William, prisoner of war (J:183, 193)

RIDLEY, Thomas, prisoner of war (D:154)

RIELY. See REILY

RILEY. See REILY

RING, Daniel, prisoner of war (H:171; J:186, 194; O:207; Q:221)

RIPKEY. See REPKEY

RIPLEY. See REPKEY

ROBINSON, David, prisoner of war (J:189; M:202; O:212; P:224)

*ROHRMANN, Augustus, deserted 21 Jun 1778 (Q:223)

ROHRMANN. See also ROMAN

ROLLINS (ROWLINS), Richard, prisoner of war (O:207; P:221)

*ROMAN, Augustin, prisoner of war (J:180)

ROMAN. See also ROHRMANN

RUEPKE. See REPKEY

SCOTT, John, prisoner of war (J:185, 196; O:206; P:222)

SELWOOD (SILWOOD), William, prisoner of war (J:186, 194; O:207; Q:221)

SEXTER (SEXTON, SIXTON), Edwzrd, prisoner of war (I:173; J:183, 193; M:198; O:208; P:218)

SIDAWAY, Thomas, discharged 23 Feb 1777 (G:168; J:181)

SILWOOD. See SELWOOD

SINCLAIR, William, prisoner of war (J:179, 189; P:224)

SMITH, John, prisoner of war (D:150; E:162; F:174; J:185, 195)

SMITH, Robert, prisoner of war (J:14, 191; M:201; O:205; P:220)

SOON?, Charles, discharged 25 Jul 1774 (A:135)

SPENCER, Walter, prisoner of war (J:189)

STANEFORD, Ephraim, prisoner of war (J:194)

*STEIR, Ernestus, Corporal, deserted 26 Feb 1778 (J:191; P:220)

STEVENS, Moses, deserted 15 Mar 1775 (B:141)

STIMSON, William, prisoner of war (P:219)

SUTHERLAND, David, discharged 25 Sep 1778 (O:206)

TAYLOR, George, discharged 25 Sep 1778 (O:214)

TAYLOR, John, prisoner of war (J:187)

TEDFORD, John, deserted 14 May 1778 (P:216)

*THEIL, Jacob, deserted 21 Jun 1777 (J:184)

THOMPSON, William, prisoner of war (A:136)

*UPEAN?, Lenard, prisoner of war (O:213)

WAID, Robert, Corporal, prisoner of war (H:172)

WARD, John, prisoner of war (F:175; J:193)

WARD, Robert, prisoner of war (E:166)

WARR, Benjamin, prisoner of war (D:150; E:162; F:174; J:185, 196)

WARREN, Francis, prisoner of war (J:177, 197; M:204; O:214)

WARREN, Thomas, prisoner of war (P:215)

WESTON, William, Drummer, prisoner of war (F:175; J:193; M:198; O:208)

WETWORTH (WITWORTH), Richard, prisoner of war (J:183, 193)

WHITE, William, discharged 23 Feb 1777 (J:178)

WILKINSON, John, discharged 24 Apr 1778 (J:178, 188; P:216)

WILKS, Henry, discharged 24 Apr 1778 (Q:223)

WILLIAMS, Thomas, prisoner of war (J:184, 191; M:201; O:205; P:220)

WILLIS, William, prisoner of war (D:148)

WINTERBOTTOM, John, prisoner of war (J:186, 194)

WISE, Stephen, discharged 24 Sep 1776 (F:176)

WITWORTH. See WETWORTH

WOODS, Samuel, deserted 12 Apr 1775 (B:138)

WRIGHT, John, discharged 24 Aug 1776 (F:169)

WRIGHT, Robert, deserted 4 Mar 1775 (B:142)

*YOUNG, Nicholas, prisoner of war (F:167; J:187; M:204; O:214; P:215)

---

1. These names were first published in Clifford Neal Smith, "Deserters, Dischargees, and Prisoners of War from the British Tenth Regiment of Foot (North Lincolnshire) During the American Revolution," National Genealogical Society Quarterly, 71:114-120 (June 1983).

2. Richard Cannon, comp., Historical Record of the Tenth, or the North Lincolnshire, Regiment of Foot, Containing An Account of the Formation of the Regiment in 1685, and Its Subsequent Services to 1847 (London:Parker, Furnivall, & Parker, 1847), p.36. A copy of this work is to be found in the Boston Public Library and has been made available by Dr. Robert Price of Lexington, Massachusetts, to whom this reporter is most grateful.

DESERTERS, DISCHARGEES, AND PRISONERS OF WAR FROM THE BRITISH FIFTEENTH REGIMENT OF FOOT (THE YORKSHIRE EAST RIDING)[1]

The Fifteenth Regiment of Foot (The Yorkshire East Riding) was an old military unit which several times had been sent to the New World to repel French encroachments on territories claimed by the British; it had participated in Canadian expeditions in 1758 and 1759; been encamped at Staten Island in 1761 and sent later that year to Barbados; had captured Martinique in 1762; fought in Habana that same year, returning to New York in 1763 and proceeding on to Canada, where it remained until returned to England in 1768. When the war with the American colonies broke out in 1776, it was not surpising that the experienced Fifteenth Regiment again was transported to North America to quell the rebels.

The itinerary of the Regiment in North America from 1776 to 1778, when it again embarked for the West Indies, is of interest to genealogical researchers, because troop movements give clues as to where soldiers are likely to have deserted or to have been discharged. Included herein are some men who may have escaped from British military control in the Caribbean islands, as well. The movements of the Fifteenth in North America were as follows:

1776   Embarked in March from Ireland for North Carolina.

Arrived at Cape Fear in April for rest and recreation after a long voyage.

On 1 June embarked for an expedition against Charleston, landing on one of the islands nearby. Unable to capture the town, the Regiment re-embarked and proceeded to Staten Island, New York.

On 22 August landed on Long Island as part of the force under Lieutenant General Clinton.

On 26 August participated in the battle at Flatbush, with only a few men wounded; thereafter, the Regiment crossed the East River and captured New York.

On 16 November the Regiment took part in the capture of Fort Washington, losing a few private soldiers killed and wounded; the unit later returned to winter quarters in New York.

1777   On 22 March a division of the Regiment participated in an expedition against Peek's Hill and again returned to New York.

On 25 April the Regiment formed part of a body of troops which embarked from New York on an expedition against Danbury, Connecticut, where American supplies were destroyed. On 27 April the Regiment skirmished with American troops and at Ridgefield the unit encountered strong opposition from General Arnold, who was routed. At the Hill of Compo, near where the British were to re-embark for New York, they were again attacked by American forces, but successfully beat them off. The following day the King's troops embarked without molestation. Eight rank and file of the Fifteenth were killed during the expedition, 16 were wounded, and two were missing.

During the summer the Regiment took the field with the army in the Jerseys without successfully raising American opposition, as they had hoped.

In August, embarking from Sandy Hook, the Regiment sailed for Chesapeake Bay as part of an army to take Philadelphia.

On 25 August the Regiment landed on the north shore of Elk River.

On 11 September the royal forces moved forward to engage the Americans at the Brandywine. The Fifteenth formed part of the column under Major General the Earl Cornwallis, who made a circuit of some miles to turn the right and gain the rear of the American army. The action was decisive, and the enemy made a precipitous retreat. During the action several men and officers were killed and wounded. After this victory, the British army continued its advance, seized Philadelphia, and took up position in and around Germantown. The Fifteenth camped to the left of the village.

On 3 October the Americans made a surprise attack on Germantown but were driven back with heavy losses. During the battle several officers of the Fifteenth Regiment were killed and 42 rank and file were wounded.

In December British troops advanced against General Washington at Whitemarsh but were repulsed. The Britsh then returned to winter quarters in Philadelphia.

1778   During the spring, the Regiment participated in several skirmishes around the countryside to open communications and to bring in supplies.

On 28 June the Regiment distinguished itself in the sharp fighting which took place near Freehold, New Jersey, during the overland march to New York.

In July the Regiment arrived in New York.

In November the Fifteenth Regiment embarked from New York to Barbados to fend off the French menace to British possessions in the Caribbean. Shortly after arrival, the Regiment was posted to St. Lucia, where it remained until June 1779; then it was sent to St. Christopher's (St. Kitts), remaining there throughout 1780.[2]

Names which appear hereinafter have been abstracted from muster rolls to be found in the Public Records Office, London, in a corpus of muster rolls denominated W.O.12, volume 3229. The muster rolls have been coded as follows, with the page number in volume 3229:

A--Philadelphia, 27 Mar 1778
B--St. Kitts, Sandy Point, 2 Jan 1781
C--Philadelphia, 6 Feb 1778
D--Brunswick [New Jersey?], 19 Apr 1777
E--Philadelphia, 23 Feb 1778
F--Piscataway, 30 Apr 1777
G--New York, 30 Dec 1776

BANKS, Thomas, deserted 14 Feb 1777 (A:104)

BELLINGHAM, Thomas, prisoner of the rebels, 24 Jul 1777? (C:115)

BROOKS, Edward, deserted 28 Dec 1777 (A:104)

CAMPBELL, Thomas, deserted 20 Jan 1777? (A:101)

COCKING, Francis, deserted 20 Dec 1780 (B:119)

COLLET, John, discharged 24 Aug 1777 (A:107)

COULTERED, John, deserted 19 Nov 1780 (B:117)

DAVIS, William, discharged 24 Jan 1777 (A:97)

DAWLINS, James, discharged 23 May 1777 (A:97)

DUNCAN, Richard?, deserted 1 Aug 1777 (A:100)

DYE, William, discharged 25 Jun 1780 (B:120)

FARRELL, Richard, deserted 2 Aug 1780 (B:118)

*FINKLER, James, deserted 24 Sep 1780 (B:122)

*FORSTER, John, deserted 10 Mar 1777 (D:93)

FOSTER, John, deserted 18 Mar 1777 (C:96)

FRANCES, Henry D., deserted 28 May or Jun 1777 (A:101)

FRASER, John, prisoner of the rebels (A:113)

HAITH, James, deserted 27 Dec 1777 (A:97, 106)

HANNEGAN, Mathew, deserted 13 Jul 1780 (B:116)

HARPER, John, prisoner (F:94)

HARRIS, Joseph, discharged 24 Aug 1777 (A:104, 114)

HOGG, John, prisoner of the rebels (C:96, 115)

JAMES, William, discharged 7 May 1777 (A:97)

JOABE?, John, deserted 7 Apr 1777 (A:97)

JOHN, Christopher, deserted 31 Aug 1780 (B:119)

JONES, James, deserted 28 Aug 1777 (A:97, 106)

KELLEY, Thomas, deserted 22 Jun 1777 (A:97)

KING, John, prisoner of the rebels (A:105, 107)

KNOX, Charles, prisoner of the enemy (A:100, 112)

LENARD (LINARD), Roger, prisoner of the enemy (A:99, 109)

McCALLUM, John, deserted 19 Dec 1777 (A:106)

MACDOWELL, Richard, deserted 15 Jul 1776 (G:95)

McLOUGHLIN, Edward, desrted 24 Aug 1780 (B:117)

MAGUIRE, James, deserted 24 Aug 1780 (B:122)

*MALTMAN (MULTMAN), Thomas, deserted 2 Sep 1777 (A:98, 110)

MOYLIN, Dennis?, prisoner of the rebels (A:105, 107)

MULTMAN. See MALTMAN

MURRAY, Edward, prisoner of the rebels (C:96, 115)

NEWBERY, Edward, discharged 24 Dec 1780 (B:116)

PEPPER, Thomas, deserted 17 Sep 1780 (B:125A)

*PETREKEN (PETREKIN), Philip, prisoner of the rebels (C:96, 115)

PHILIPS (PHILLIPS), Robert, discharged 24 Jul 1777 (A:97, 106)

PRESCOTT, Frederick Augustus, discharged 24 Jul 1777 (A:103, 113)

PRESCOTT, Robert, discharged 24 Jul 1777 (A:101, 108)

PRESCOTT, William, discharged 24 Jul 1777 (A:103, 113)

REID, Duncan, deserted 1 Aug 1777 (A:122)

ROACH, William, deserted 24 Sep 1780 (B:122)

ROSS, John, discharged 29 Jul 1777 (A:103, 113)

*SANTON, Henry, prisoner (G:86); deserted 21 Nov 1780 (B:116)

SNOW? (*STROUS?), Daberough (Daderough), deserted 8 Dec 1777 (A:101, 108)

WALSH, Michael, deserted? 23 Feb 1777 (A:98)

WATKINS, Edward, deserted 29 Aug 1777 (A:104, 114)

WHITAKER, William, prisoner of the rebels (E:111)

WOLDEN, John, deserted 31 Jan 1778 (A:114)

---

* Possibly a German, of which there were many in British units during the American revolution.

1. These names were first published in the National Genealogical Society Quarterly 70:15-17 (March 1982).

2. Information taken from Richard Cannon, comp., Historical Record of the Fifteenth, or, The Yorkshire East Riding, Regiment of Foot, ... (London: Parker, Furnival, & Parker, 1848).

DESERTERS, DISCHARGEES, AND PRISONERS OF WAR FROM THE
BRITISH SIXTEENTH REGIMENT OF FOOT
(BEDFORDSHIRE OR BUCKINGHAMSHIRE)[1]

During the American Revolution, the British Sixteenth Regiment of Foot was known as the Bedfordshire Regiment; in August of 1782 it became known as the Buckingham Regiment. Muster rolls preserved in the Public Records Office, London (War Office 12, Volume 3320) are listed unter the latter title.

In this series it has been hypothesized that, if the researcher knows the wartime history of a regiment, the places of desertion, discharge, or internment can be determined--a factor in predicting the general region in which a deserting soldier might first turn up in American records. Considerable experience now teaches that the hypothesis is difficult to test, because so few deserters can be identified in the 1790 federal censuses, for reasons still unclear. In any event the places of settlement of deserting soldiers from the Sixteenth Regiment would be particularly difficult to predict, because the Regiment was widely dispersed throughout what became the southern portion of the United States almost from its arrival on this continent. The history of the Regiment in North America is as follows:

1767   The Regiment embarked from Ireland and, upon arrival, was stationed at Pensacola, Florida, a region ceded by the Spaniards to Great Britain in 1763 in exchange for "the Havannah" (Cuba).

1768   Detachments from the Regiment were then detailed to various military stations in East and West Florida.

1776   The Regiment was withdrawn from Florida to join the British army at New York under Lieutenant-General Sir William Howe, but the necessity of having a small force in the ceded Spanish province soon became evident, and the Regiment received orders to return to Pensacola. Again, detachments were sent to various posts in East and West Florida and Georgia.

1779   The court of Spain commenced hostilities against Great Britain, and Don Bernardo de Galvez, governor of the Spanish province of Louisiana, suddenly invaded the British territories on the banks of the Mississippi. Lieutenant-Colonel Dickson of the Sixteenth Regiment, who commanded the troops in that district, being unable to oppose the invading Spanish army, withdrew to Baton Rouge, where he caused a redoubt to be constructed. It was scarcely completed, when the Spanish advanced in force against this post, investing it on 12 September. On 21 September, after much fighting, the British surrendered. The garrison, consisting of detachments of the Sixteenth and Sixtieth British regiments and the Waldeck German regiment, was sent as prisoners of war to New Orleans, and afterwards exchanged.

At about the same time, French forces under Comte d'Estaing approached the port of Savannah, where another detachment of the Sixteenth Regiment, commanded by Major Graham, formed part of the force under Major-General Prevost which defended that place. On 24 September Major Graham and his detachment sallied against the French and their American allies under General Lincoln and "artfully drew the enemy into a snare, by which the French and Americans fired on each other, and had fifty men killed before the mistake was discovered." Before daylight on 9 October, the French and Americans made a desperate effort to capture Savannah by storm, but they were repulsed at every point with severe loss. They afterwards raised the siege and retired.

1781   Mustering a force of over 9000 men, the Spaniards under de Galvez began an attack directly against Pensacola, defended by about 1200 soldiers of the Sixteenth Regiment. On 8 May, after an explosion destroyed their powder magazine, the British commander, Major-General John Campbell, agreed to surrender on condition that the garrison should march out with the honors of war and be sent to British territory. The garrison was not to serve against the Spanish.

1782   The Regiment was recalled to Great Britain, arriving in England in March.[2]

Ethnically, the Sixteenth Regiment was both British and German. Many of the Germans can be identified, despite the anglicized spelling of their surnames. As one might imagine, many German soldiers deserted, being hired mercenaries with no particular loyalty to Great Britain. Normally, the German soldiers deserted in groups:

1778 Dec 29-31: Collier [Koehler?], Fide (Veit?), Silligh [Selig?], Haller, Flack

1779 Oct 9, 24: King [Koenig?], Horn, Olkers, Swantz [Schwantz]

1780 May 24   Cobbushack, Ganter

1781 Apr 13, 20: Uss, Heater

1781 May 15, 18: Groff [Graff], Stineman [Steinmann], Weymer [Weimar], Sheeler [Schueler?], Winegar [Essig?], Ulbright [Ulbrecht?], Gould [Gold]

As a general observation, the desertions of British soldiers were sporadic, often solitary, and rarely with German soldiers of their Regiment.

Information hereinafter has been extracted from three muster rolls to be found in the Public Records Office, London, War Office 12, volume 3320. The page number is also given:

   A--St. Augustine, Florida, 29 Jan 1778
   B--New Town, Long Island, 3 Sep 1781
   C--Leeds, England, 21 Sep 1782

ABBOTT, Lawrence, discharged 2 Aug 1778 (B:49)

ATKINSON, Robert, Sergeant, prisoner in the Havannah [Cuba] (C:79)

BARKER, William, Captain, prisoner in the Havannah [Cuba] C:68)

BERGMANN, Anthony [probably German], deserted 27 May 1781 (B:59, 62, 67)

BROWNGATE, Mathew (or Michael), deserted 14 May 1781 (B:51, 54, 57, 63, 65)

BURK, John, deserted 6 Oct 16780 (B:53, 58, 60)

CARRIGUE (CARRIQUE), Richard, discharged 25 Aug 1781, thereafter working for W. Porter, Deputy Commissary [in New York?] (B:53, 58, 60, 66)

CARTER, James, deserted 29 Dec 1780 (B:62, 67)

COBBUSHACK, Francis [probably German], deserted 24 May 1780 (B:54, 57)

COLL, John [KOEHL, possible German surname], deserted 11 Dec 1778 (B:51)

COLLIER?, Frederick [KOEHLER, probable German surname], deserted 29 Dec 1778 (B:53)

COOPER, Theop[hilus?], Sergeant, prisoner of war in the Havannah [Cuba] (C:78)

COWPER, John, Sergeant, prisoner of war with the enemy (C:69)

DELANEY, John, Corporal, prisoner of war with the Spaniards (C:70)

DOWELL (DOWELE), John, Drummer, deserted 25 Aug or Oct 1780 (B:49, 62)

DRESMIRE?, John [possibly German], deserted 11 Jun 1778 (B:50)

ENNIS, Thomas, deserted 30 Aug 1778 (B:50)

FIDE, Jacob [VEIT probable German surname], deserted 29 Dec 1778 (B:53)

FLACK, Andrew [probably German], deserted 31 Dec 1778 (B:50, 55)

GANTER, Nicholas (or Neil)[probably German], deserted 25 May 1780 (B:54, 57)

GERA, Christian [probably German], deserted 2 Aug 1778 (B:51)

GOULD, Michael [GOLD possible German surname], deserted 24 May 1781 (B:53, 58, 60, 66)

GROFF, Ferdinand, Corporal [GRAF, possible German surname], deserted 4 or 18 May 1781 (B:55, 56, 61)

HALLER, Jacob (or Jack) [probably German], deserted 31 Dec 1778 (B:50, 55)

HAMILTON, John, Adjutant, prisoner of war of Spain, taken at Baton Rouge (B:53, 58, 60, 66)

HAMILTON, John, Ensign, prisoner of war of Spain, taken at Baton Rouge (B:53, 58, 60, 66) [probably the same officer as above]

HAWKSFORD, Samuel, Drummer, prisoner of war in the Havannah [Cuba] (C:68)

HEATER, David [HEIZER? HAEDER? possible German surname], deserted 20 Apr 1781 (B:59, 62, 67)

HORN, Christian [probably German], deserted 24 Oct 1779 (B:49, 52)

HYNES, Anthony [HEINZ, possible German surname], prisoner of war with the Spaniards (B:56, 61, 64)

JOHNSTONE, Robert, discharged 2 Aug 1778 (B:51)

KEITH, John, Drummer, prisoner of war with the Spaniards (C:70)

KENEDY, John, Drummer, prisoner of war with the enemy (C:72)

KENNY, John, Corporal, prisoner of war in the Havannah [Cuba] (C:68)

KENT, Patt[rick], prisoner of war (A:48)

KING, Joseph, deserted 9 Oct 1778 (or 1779) (B:49, 52)

LAWLESS, Henry, Corporal, prisoner of war with the rebels (C:71)

LAWSON, James, deserted 25 May 1781 (B:59, 62, 67)

LEIDEN? (SEIDEN?), Henry, Sergeant [possibly German], prisoner of war at the Havannah [Cuba] (C:76)

LELAND, Thomas, Corporal, prisoner of war in the Havannah [Cuba] (C:68)

LENDIGREN, Nathaniel, Lieutenant [LUENDGREN, possible German surname], prisoner of war in the Havannah [Cuba] (C:68)

LOW, Addison, Quartermaster, prisoner of war of Spain, taken at Baton Rouge, later on parole with the regiment (B:53, 58; 60, 66; C:69)

McCONNEL, James, Corporal, prisoner of war with the rebels (C:71)

McGILL, Henry, Corporal, prisoner of war in the Havannah [Cuba] (C:68)

McGUIRE, Philip, Corporal, deserted 4 May 1781 (B:56, 61)

McWILLIAMS, John, deserted 28 Nov 1778 (B:51)

MATHEWS, Mathias, discharged 2 Aug 1778 (B:49)

MONAGHAN, Edward, Sergeant, prisoner of war with the enemy (C:72)

MORGAN, Thomas, deserted 11 Aug 1780 or 1781 (B:52, 59,.62)

MORTON, David, prisoner of war with the Spaniards (B:54, 57, 63, 65)

MULREMAN, Martin [probably German], deserted 24 Aug 1778 (B:51)

MURPHY, Hugh, deserted 28 Jul 1777 (A:46)

NASH, Giles, Drummer, prisoner of war with the enemy (C:77)

NEWLANDS, John, Lieutenant, prisoner of war in the Havannah [Cuba] (C:79)

OLKERS, Christian [probably German], deserted 24 Oct 1779 (B:49, 52)

O'NEIL, John, discharged 2 Aug 1778 (B:51)

OTT, George, Sergeant, prisoner of war with the rebels (C:71)

PIERCE, John, deserted 14 May 1781 (B:55, 61, 64)

PIEROTT, Francis, discharged 12 Feb 1778 or 1779 (B:49, 52)

PROCTOR?, Robert, Drummer, discharged 23 Jul 1778 (B:49)

QUIGLEY, Edward, deserted 1 Dec 1778 (B:50)

REED, Henry, deserted 29 May 1781 (B:59, 62, 67)

REEDER, Thomas, deserted 25 May 1781 (B:49,·52, 59, 62, 67)

RICHARDS, Joseph, discharged 2 Aug 1778 (B:50)

SAPLE (SAPPLE), Philip [possibly German], prisoner of war with the rebels (B:50, 55, 56, 61, 64)

SCHUELER. See SHEELER

SCHWANTZ. See SWANTZ

SEIDEN. See LEIDEN

SELIG. See SILLIGH

SHANNON, John, Sergeant, prisoner of war with the rebels (C:74)

SHEELER, John [SCHUELER, probable German surname], deserted 18 May 1781 (B:51, 54, 57, 63, 65)

SILLIGH, Frederick [SELIG, probable German surname], deserted 31 Dec 1778 (B:50, 55)

SMITH, William, deserted 25 May 1781 (B:62, 67)

SNELLOCK, Thomas, discharged 11 May 1781 (B:67)

STANLEY, Joseph, discharged 11 May 1781 (B:67)

STINEMAN, Andrew [STEINMANN, probably German surname], deserted 14 May 1781 (B:50, 55, 56, 61, 64)

STRAHAN, James, prisoner of war at the Havannah [Cuba] (C:75)

SWANTZ, Christian [SCHWANTZ, probable German surname], deserted 24 Oct 1779 (B:49, 52)

THOMAS, Edmund or Edwin, Surgeon, prisoner of war of Spain, taken at Baton Rouge (B:53, 58, 60, 66; C:69)

THOMPSON, James, Corporal, prisoner of war with the rebels (C:71)

ULBRIGHT, John [ULBRECHT, ULBRICHT, probable German surname], deserted 18 May 1781 (B:50, 55, 56, 61, 64)

USS, Francis [possibly German], deserted 13 Apr 1781 (B:59, 62, 67)

WADMAN, Praise, Sergeant, discharged 31 Aug 1781 (B:56, 61)

WELSHMAN, John, Sergeant, prisoner of war in the Havannah [Cuba] (C:68)

WEYMER, Henry [WEIMAR, probable German surname], deserted 18 May 1781 (B:59, 62, 67)

WILKINSON, James, Sergeant, prisoner of war with the Spaniards (C:70)

WILLIAMS, Edward, deserted 25 May 1781 (B:49, 52, 59, 62, 67)

WILLIAMS, Henry, Corporal, prisoner of war with the enemy (C:72)

WILLIS, Samuel, Sergeant, discharged 1 Jul 1777 (A:46).

WILLSON, Thomas, Drummer?, prisoner of war with the enemy (C:77)

WILSON, John, Drummer, prisoner of war with the enemy (C:72)

WILSON, Thomas, Drummer, prisoner of war with the Spaniards (B:49, 62) [possibly the same man as Thomas WILLSON above]

WINEGAR (WINNEGAR), George [possibly ESSIG (translation) or WEINESSIG, both German surnames], deserted 18 May 1781 (B:54, 57, 63, 65)

ZIERECK, Conrad [probably German], prisoner of war with the Spaniards (B:56)

---

1. Originally published as an article of the same title in the National Genealogical Society Quarterly, 74:279-282.

2. Information taken from Richard Cannon, comp., Historical Record of the Sixteenth, or Bedfordshire, Regiment of Foot: Containing an Account of the Formation of the Regiment in 1688, and of Its Subsequent Services to 1848 (London: Parker, Furnivall, & Parker, 1848).

DESERTERS, DISCHARGEES, AND PRISONERS OF WAR FROM THE
BRITISH THIRD REGIMENT OF FOOT
(EAST KENT OR THE BUFFS)[1]

The Regiment of Buffs, formerly designated The Holland Regiment, possesses the privilege of marching unhindered through the City of London with drums beating--a relic of Elizabethan days.

The list of prisoners of war hereinafter has been taken from muster rolls in the Public Records Office, London, (War Office 12, volume 2106). The history of the Regiment in North America is as follows:[2]

1775 During the early part of the war between Great Britain and the American colonies, the Regiment was employed on home service; but after France and Spain had joined with the revolted Americans, and the armies and fleets of the two crowns were employed against Great Britain, the Buffs were called from their quarters in Ireland to cross the Atlantic Ocean, and to take part in the warfare carried on against the insurgent provincials.

1781 The regiment embarked from Ireland in March 1781 and arrived at Charleston, South Carolina, on 3 June and was soon engaged in active operations.

At the moment when the Buffs arrived on the American continent, the enemy was besieging Ninety-Six, a village so called from being that number of miles from Kecowee in the Cherokee country; like other villages on the frontiers of the colonies, it was originally surrounded with a stockade for the protection of the inhabitants against the sudden assaults of the Indians; some new works were added in 1780 and in the early part of 1781, and was garrisoned by several detachments under Lieutenant Colonel Cruger. On the 7th of June the flank companies of the Third, forming part of a small force placed under the orders of Lieutenant Colonel Lord Rawdon, advanced with all possible expedition from Charleston for the relief of the besieged fortress, and after a long and harassing march, arrived at Ninety-Six on the 21st of the same month. Meanwhile, the Americans had raised the siege and retired across the river Saluda; and, notwithstanding the fatigue which the king's troops had already undergone, and the excessive heat of the weather, they pushed forward in pursuit on the same evening. The Americans fled with great rapidity and were followed by the English as far as the banks of the Enoree, when the latter, finding it in vain to pursue so fleet an enemy, returned towards Ninety-Six.

The flank companies of the Third Regiment subsequently proceeded to the Congaree, a considerable river formed by the confluence of the Saluda and Broad rivers, where Lord Rawdon expected to be reinforced by troops from Charleston; but soon after his arrival at this part of the country he ascertained that the American general Green was advancing with an army to cut off the British detachment, when he instantly retired; and the troops forced, at noon-day, and in face of the enemy, their passage over a creek, the bridges of which were broken down and the fords guarded by Lee's American legion, and effected their retreat to the town of Orangeburg, situated on the north branch of the Edisto, where the detachment was joined by the remainder of the Third from Charleston, commanded by Lieutenant Colonel Alexander Stewart.

The American commander, finding the detachment, by a daring and spirited movement, had extricated itself from the danger to which it was exposed, advanced to the vicinity of the British camp near Orangeburg, and reconnoitred the position with his cavalry; but, instead of preparing for an attack, he retired during the night towards the Congaree, and subsequently to the high hills of Santee; having previously sent out parties to attack several detached posts occupied by the British troops, who were much harassed with the defence of an extensive frontier.

After the retreat of the Americans, the Buffs, and other corps under the orders of Lieutenant Colonel Stewart, advanced to the Congaree and encamped near the junction of that river with the Wateree.

The American army was soon afterwards reinforced with troops from North Carolina, and being now greatly superior in numbers to the royal forces under Lieutenant Colonel Stewart of the Third Regiment, who had taken post on Colonel Thompson's estate near McCord's ferry on the Congaree, General Green resolved to advance against his opponents. When the Americans advanced, the British were almost without provisions; a supply was on its way from Charleston, but escorts could not be spared lest the remainder should be too weak to resist the enemy; the troops, therefore, retreated about forty miles to a place called Eutaw Springs, where they halted.

They were, at this period, without bread, and owing to the disaffection of a great portion of the inhabitants to the British cause, no information of the approach of the American army had been received, consequently, at an early hour on the morning of the 8th of September, about fifty of the Buffs, with small parties from other corps, were sent out to search the fields for potatoes, and while thus employed they were surprised by the American army, several were killed and wounded, and the remainder made prisoners. Lieutenant Edward Silvester, who commanded the Buffs, was dangerously wounded.

An alarm of the approach of the enemy was, at the same time, given by the outposts; the remainder of the regiment was soon under arms, and the troops formed in order of battle about two miles in front of their camp, occupying the heights near Eutaw Springs, with the Buffs on the left of the line. About nine o'clock the Americans diverged upon the grounds in front of the British position and commenced the attack with great fury. The royal forces,

1781 though inferior in numbers, sustained the first onset with admirable firmness; a fierce conflict of musketry ensued, and both armies displayed great gallantry. The Buffs repulsed and drove back the troops in their front, but advancing too forward in the pursuit, the regiment became exposed to the superior numbers of the enemy, and it was over powered and driven back with loss; it, however, rallied. A sharp fire of musketry blazed among the trees, charges with bayonet became frequent, many instances of valour were displayed by both parties, and the sixty-third and sixty-four regiments particularly distinguished themselves; but the superior numbers of the enemy rendered it necessary for the British troops to retire nearer their camp ground.

When the retrograde movement was commenced, a large party took possession of a strong brick house of three stories, with its adjoining offices, another party lodged itself in an almost impenetrable coppice of rugged underwood, whie a third possessed itself of a palisadoed garden; and as the Americans came forward with great spirit and vigour, these parties opened their fire, and the storm of battle soon raged with greater fury than before. The enemy brought forward four pieces of cannon to play on the brick house, and Colonel Washington attempted attempted to force the coppice, but every effort was ineffectual. Incessant peals of musketry from the windows poured destruction upon the Americans--Colonel Washington was wounded and taken prisoner--the Buffs had gained their appointed station on the left and were opening their fire--and the flank battalion, wheeling round, took the enemy in the rear; when the Americans, finding all their efforts vain, retired, leaving two brass field pieces, and about sixty men, in the hands of the British.

The commander, Lieutenant Colonel Stewart, of the Third Regiment, observed in his despatch: "The glory of the day would have been much more complete, had not the want of cavalry prevented me from taking the advantage which the gallantry of my infantry threw in my way." Both commanders, however, claimed the victory; the American, because of the retreat of the British during the action; and the British, because of the retreat of the Americans at the close of the action.

The loss of the regiment at the battle of Eutaw Springs was Lieutenant Buckwith, one serjeant, one drummer, and twenty-seven rank and file killed; Brevet Major Hon. John Leslie, three serjeants, and seventy-four rank and file wounded; and Lieutenant Douglas Hamilton, two serjeants, one drummer, and seventy rank and file taken prisoners.

The regiment passed the night after the action, and the following day, on the ground, and in the evening retired with the remainder of the army to Monk's Corner; and the Americans withdrew soon afterwards to their former camp on the high hills of Santee; both armies having suffered so severely that neither was in a condition to act offensively against the other.

1782 A new line of posts was afterwards established by the British; and a desultory warfare was carried on by detachments, without being attended with very important results. At length King George III was induced to concede the independence of the United States of America; and, while the treaty of peace was negotiating, a suspension of hostilities took place, and the Buffs proceeded from South Carolina to the island of Jamaica. The regiment remained at Jamaica from 1782 until the spring of 1790.

***

There appear to be no extant muster rolls dating from the 1781-1782 period, when the Third Regiment was in the American colonies; a diligent check for them was made in War Office 12, volume 2105, which is apparently complete until near the time of the regiment's departure from Ireland in 1781. All musters in subsequent volume 2106 are from 1783, probably all taken in Jamaica, but seemingly reflecting action taken in South Carolina before the regiment's departure for Jamaica in 1782. Note, however, that some prisoners of war in America, listed hereinafter, were captured <u>before</u> the Third Regiment reached the New World. It is thought that they pertain to men who had originally been in other British regiments and reassigned to the Third Regiment only <u>after</u> their release from American captivity following the peace settlement in 1783. The rolls cited hereinafter are as follows:

    A--Fort Augusta [Jamaica?], 24 Jul 1783
    B--No place given [probably Jamaica], Aug 1783
    C--No place given [ditto], 21 Aug 1783
    D--Kingston [Jamaica], 24 Aug 1783

Following the muster roll designation, the page number in volume 2106 is given, e.g., A:1 means roll A with name to be found on page 1 of volume 2106.

ARBINSON?, James. <u>See</u> James ORBISON

BOND, Benjamin, prisoner of war, 16 Jan 1778 (A:05; D:13)

BOWYERS (BOYERS), MATTHEW, prisoner of war, 17 Nov 1779 (A:04; C:12) [possibly German]

BRADBURRY, George, prisoner of war (A:02)

CHALMERS, James, prisoner of war (A:05)

CONNALLY (CONALY), Arthur, prisoner of war, 17 May 1778 (A:07; D:16)

CONNALY, Thomas, prisoner of war (A:04)

CONNELY, Henry, prisoner of war, 10 Jan 1779 (C:12)

COTTER, William, prisoner of war (A:09)

CREATON, James, prisoner of war, 08 Feb 1780 (A:06; B:15)

CRUTCHELL, William, prisoner of war (A:07)

DONAGHER (DONAHER), Peter, prisoner of war, 22 Jul 1778 (A:05; D:13)

DONALD? (DONALL?), Robert, prisoner of war (A:04)

DONALDSON, Joseph, prisoner of war, 17 Dec 1760! (A:10; D:19)

DROPE (DROUPE), William, prisoner of war, 19 Jan 1780 (A:01; B:11)

ELLIOTT (ELITT), Thomas, prisoner of war, 01 Jan 1779 (A:04; C:12)

ELLIOTT (ELETT), William, prisoner of war, 01 Feb 1779 (A:06; B:15)

FISH, Simon, prisoner of war, 27 Dec 1777 (A:05; D:13)

FITZSIMMONS, Robert, prisoner of war (A:03)

FLYNN (FLINN), George, prisoner of war, 28 Jun 1777 (A:09; D:17)

FRAZER (FRAYZER), Robert, prisoner of war, 06 Dec 1777 (A:07; D:16)

FUGUARD, Thomas, prisoner of war (A:03)

GIBS, John, prisoner of war (A:10)

GRANT, Frederick, deserted 24 Jun 1782 (A:04)

GRANT, Patrick, prisoner of war (A:10)

GROOM, William, prisoner of war (A:10)

HADWIN, Francis, prisoner of war, 24 Jun 1776 (D:17)

HARDWIN, Thomas, prisoner of war (A:09)

HARISE? (HASSE?), George, prisoner of war (A:01)

HAYES, George, prisoner of war, 12 Apr 1780? or 1776? (A:01?; B:11) [possibly the same man as George HASSE, above]

HENESSEY, John, prisoner of war, 11 May 1778 (C:12)

HIGGISON (HIGASON), Stewart, prisoner of war, 17 Mar 1776 (A:05; D:13)

HITCHCOCK, Thomas, prisoner of war (A:06)

HUMPAGE, Samuel, prisoner of war (A:05)

HUNTER, William, prisoner of war, 20 May 1778 (A:08; B:14)

KAY? (THAY?), James, prisoner of war, 01 Jan 1774! (D:19)

KENNEY, John, prisoner of war (A:04)

LEONARD (LENORD), William, prisoner of war, 10 Oct 1779 (A:03; D:20)

LOGAN, John, prisoner of war (A:08)

LOWTHER, Robert, prisoner of war, 11 Jan 1777 (A:02; D:18)

MALLONEY, Thomas, prisoner of war (A:04)

McALIER? [McALAN?], James, prisoner of war, 12 Jun 1778 (A:04; C:12)

McALIER (McALEER), Patt (Pall), prisoner of war, 28 Sep 1778 (A:04; C:12)

McBRYAN, John, prisoner of war, 01 Nov 1778 (A:01; B:11)

McCALLEY (McCAWLEY), Richard, prisoner of war, 11 Mar 1776 (A:08; B:14)

McDONALD, Robert, prisoner of war, 30 Mar 1777 (C:12)

McDONAUGH (McDONOGH), John, prisoner of war, 28 May 1778 (A:02; D:18)

McDOULE, James, prisoner of war, 19 Jul 1778 (D:18)

McDOULL, John, prisoner of war (A:07) [possibly the same man as James McDoule, above]

McMULLAN, James, prisoner of war (A:01) [possibly the same man as James McMullen, below]

McMULLAN, Thomas, prisoner of war (A:07)

McMULLEN, James, prisoner of war, 23 Apr 1778 (B:11)

McMULLEN, James, prisoner of war, 19 Mar 1780 (D:16)

McNAMEE, Patrick, prisoner of war (A:01)

McPHERSON (McPHARSON), James, prisoner of war, 20 Apr 1778 (A:05; D:13)

MOORE, John, prisoner of war (A:05)

MORGAN, James, prisoner of war, 10 Sep 1774! (D:13)

MORGAN, Joseph, drummer, prisoner of war (A:05)

MORROUGH, John, prisoner of war, 04 Apr 1776 (A:03; D:20)

MULLHOLAND, William, prisoner of war, 11 May 1778 (A:03; D:20)

MURPHEY, Thomas, prisoner of war (A:06)

MURPHY, John, prisoner of war, 02 May 1777 (B:15)

MURPHY, Robert, corporal, prisoner of war, 09 Aug 1777 (A:08; B:14)

NELSON, John, prisoner of war (A:04)

O'NEAL (O'NEILL), James, prisoner of war, 07 Jan 1769! (A:09; D:17)

O'NEAL, Roger, prisoner of war, 13 Jan 1778 (A:01; B:11)

ORBISON (ARBINSON; ORBINSON), James, prisoner of war, 27 Feb 1778 (A:05; D:13)

PENNON, Thomas, prisoner of war (A:03)

PRICE, Charles, prisoner of war, 17 Mar 1780 (A:03; D:20)

QUINN, Neal (Neill), prisoner of war, 01 Jan 1778 (A:04; C:12)

RAY, James, prisoner of war (A:10)

REEDA (REIDA), James, prisoner of war, 10 Jul 1778 (A:10; D:19)

ROBINSON, William, prisoner of war (A:10)

ROSS, William, prisoner of war, 31 May 1774! (A:09; D:17)

SMITH, Patt, prisoner of war, 10 Jul 1776 (A:03; D:20)

SMITH, Robert, prisoner of war, 05 May 1778 (A:07; D:16)

SMITH, William, prisoner of war (A:02)

SUMMERS, Thomas, prisoner of war, 10 Apr 1759! (A:06; B:15)

TAYLOR, James, prisoner of war, 16 Dec 1776 (D:18) [might be the same man as John Taylor, below]

TAYLOR, John, prisoner of war (A:02)

THAY, James. See James KAY

WALSH, Robert, prisoner of war, 01 Jan 1780 (A:03; D:20)

WEST, John, prisoner of war, 26 Sep 1777 (A:03; D:20)

WHITE, Robert, prisoner of war, 02 Feb 1778 (A:01; B:11)

WOODS, Samuel, prisoner of war, 26 Sep 1777 (A:03; D:20)

WRIGHT, Daniel, prisoner of war, 10 Aug 1774! (A:10; D:19)

---

1. The records of this regiment have not been published previously.

2. Quoted verbatim from Richard Cannon, comp., <u>Historical Records of the Third Regiment of Foot, or the Buffs, Formerly Designated the Holland Regiment, Containing an Account of Its Origin in the Reign of Queen Elizabeth and of Its Subsequent Services to 1838</u> (London: Longman, Orme, & Co., 1839).

A DESERTER FROM THE BRITISH NINTH REGIMENT OF FOOT (EAST NORFOLK)[1]

Hereinafter recorded is the name of one deserter from the British Ninth Regiment of Foot. This writer regrets that, during a research trip to the Public Records Office, London, he did not have time to analyze the numerous muster rolls for this regiment while it was stationed in Isle de Jesus, Canada. The rolls are to be found in a corpus of manuscripts entitled War Office 12, volume 2653. The Ninth Regiment is of some importance to American genealogical researchers, because it was captured at Saratoga and became a part of the so-called Convention Army, prisoners of war in Virginia until 1781. The history of the regiment through 1776, during which the deserter fled, was as follows:[2]

1775 The regiment was stationed in Ireland when the British colonies in North America broke their allegiance and openly resisted the royal authority. During the winter of 1775, Quebec was besieged by an American army, a fortress defended under Lieutenant General Guy Carleton.

1776 In April the Ninth Regiment of Foot, commanded by Lieutenant Colonel John Hill, embarked from Ireland and sailed for Canada with other forces under Major General Burgoyne. The regiment arrived in the river St. Lawrence in the beginning of June, and the Americans having raised the siege of Quebec and retired towards Montreal, it sailed up the river and took part in the operations by which the Americans were driven from Canada. After the performance of this service, it went into cantonments for a short period among the Canadian peasantry, and it passed the winter on the Isle of Jesus, at La Praire, St. Luce Recollect, and St. Genevieve.

SMYTH, James, deserted 21 Sep 1776, according to a muster roll, dated 25 Feb 1777, from Verchere. [Presumably, the desertion would have been in Canada.][page 244]

---

1. No research into the records of this regiment have been published previously.

2. Information taken from the official War Office regimental history, Richard Cannon, comp., <u>Historical Record of the Ninth, or the East Norfolk, Regiment of Foot, Containing an Account of the Formation of the Regiment in 1685, and Its Subsequent Services to 1847</u> (London: Parker, Furnivall, & Parker, 1848).

Surname Index

ABBOTT, 9
ALLEN, 2
ANNALY, 2
ANSON, 2
ANTWISTLE, 2
ARBINSON. See ORBISON
ASHWORTH, 2
ASKWORTH, 2
ASWORTH, 2
ATKINS, 2
ATKINSON, 9
BALL, 2
BAMFIELD, 2
BANKS, 7
BARKER, 9
BARNETT, 2
BARNFIELD, 2
BELK, 2
BELLINGHAM, 7

BENNET, 2
BERGER, 2
BERGMANN, 9
BEYER, 2
BILK. See BELK
BOND, 12
BONER, 2
BONNER, 2
BOWYERS, 12
BOYD, 2
BOYERS, 12
BRADBURRY, 12
BRADSHWAW, 2
BRIEN, 2
BROOKS, 7
BROWNGATE, 9
BURK, 9
CAMPBELL, 2, 7
CAMPLE, 2
CANITZ, 2
CANNON, 2
CARELTON, 2
CARELTON. See also CHARELTON
CARRIGUE, 9
CARRIQUE, 9
CARSON, 2
CARTER, 9
CASEY. See KEACY
CHALMERS, 2, 12
CHAMBERS, 2
CHARELTON, 2
CHARLETON, 2
CHARLTON, 2
CLAIN. See KLANE
CLARK, 2

CLINARD, 2
COBBUSHACK, 8, 9
COCKING, 7
COLL, 9
COLLET, 7
COLLIER, 8, 9
COLLINS, 2
COMMINS, 2
CONALY, 12
CONITZ. See CANITZ
CONNALLY, 12
CONNELY, 12
CONNERS, 2
COOK, 2
COOPER, 2, 9
COTTER, 12
COULTERED, 7
COVENEY, 2
COVENY, 2
COWPER, 9
CREATON, 12
CRISSWELL, 2
CRUSE, 2
CRUTCHELL, 12
CURREN, 2
CURRIN, 2
DAGG, 2
DAMMON, 2
DAMON, 2
DAVIS, 2, 7
DAWLINS, 7
DEAN, 2
DELANEY, 9
DICKMAN, 2
DONAGHER, 13
DONAHER, 13

DONALD, 13
DONALDSON, 13
DONALL, 13
DOWDS, 2
DOWELE, 9
DOWELL, 9
DRESMIRE, 9
DROPE, 13
DROUPE, 13
DUNCAN, 7
DUNLAP, 2
DUNMAID, 2
DUNN, 2
DYE, 7
ELETT, 13
ELITT, 13
ELLIOT, 3
ELLIOTT, 3, 13
ELLIS, 3
ENNIS, 9
ESSIG. See WINEGAR
EVANS, 3
FAIR, 3
FAIRLEY, 3
FARMER, 3
FARRELL, 7
FIDE, 8, 9
FINKLER, 7
FISH, 13
FITZSIMMONS, 13
FLACK, 8, 9
FLINN, 13
FLYNN, 13
FORKE, 3
FORKEY, 3
FORSTER, 7

FOSTER, 7
FOWLER, 3
FRANCES, 7
FRANKS, 3
FRAPWELL, 3
FRASER, 7
FRAYZER, 13
FRAZER, 13
FUGUARD, 13
GALPIN. See GULPIN
GANTER, 8, 9
GARDINER, 3
GARVEY, 3
GEFFERY, 3
GERA, 9
GIBS, 13
GILLROY, 3
GILPIN. See GULPIN
GILROY, 3
GLENN, 3
GOADBROTH, 3
GOLD, 8, 9
GOULD, 8, 9
GRAF(F), 8, 9
GRANT, 3, 13
GROFF, 8, 9
GROOM, 13
GULPIN, 3
GUTBROT. See GOADBROTH
HADWIN, 13
HAEDER, 9
HAILS, 3
HAITH, 7
HALDON, 3
HALES, 3
HALL, 3

HALLER, 8, 9
HALLES, 3
HALLES. See HAILS
HALSINDINE, 3
HAMILTON, 9
HANDS, 3
HANIFORD, 3
HANKEY, 3
HANNEGAN, 7
HANNIFORD, 3
HARDEN, 3
HARDIN, 3
HARDON, 3
HARDWIN, 13
HARISE, 13
HARPER, 7
HARRIS, 7
HASKINDINE, 3
HASKINDINE. See HALSINDINE; HELSENBERGER; HELSENDEGN
HASSE, 13
HAWKSFORD, 9
HAYES, 13
HEAGUE, 3
HEATER, 8, 9
HEIMPEL, 3
HEINZ, 9
HEIZER, 9
HELSENDEGER, 3
HELSENDEGN, 3
HENESSEY, 13
HICKEY, 3
HIGASON, 13
HIGGASON, 13
HIMPLES, 3

HIRTH, 3
HITCHCOCK, 13
HOEFER. See HUFFER
HOGG, 7
HOLBROCK, 3
HOLBROOK, 3
HOLMES, 3
HORN, 8, 9
HUFFER, 3
HUGHES, 3
HUMPAGE, 13
HUNTER, 13
HUTCHINSON, 3
HYNES, 9
INGRAM, 3
JACKSON, 3
JAEGER. See JAGGER
JAGGAR, 3
JAGGER, 3
JAMES, 7
JEFFERY. See GEFFERY
JENKINS, 3
JOABE, 7
JOHN, 7
JOHNSTONE, 9
JONES, 7
JUNG. See YOUNG
KANITZ. See CANITZ
KAY, 13
KEACY, 3
KEITH, 9
KELLER, 3
KELLEY, 3, 7
KELLY, 3, 4
KENADY, 4, 9

KENEDY, 9
KENNEY, 13
KENNY, 9
KENT, 9
KING, 7, 8, 9
KLANE, 4
KNOX, 7
KOEHLER, 8, 9
KOENIG, 8
KONITZ. See CANITZ
KUBICEK; KUBITSCHECK. See COBBUSHACK
LAMPRECHT. See LAMPRIGHT
LAMPRIGHT, 4
LAWLESS, 9
LAWSON, 9
LEE, 4
LEIDEN, 9
LELAND, 9
LENARD, 7
LENDIGREN, 9
LENORD, 13
LEONARD, 13
LEWIS, 4
LINARD, 7
LOGAN, 13
LOW, 9
LOWTHER, 13
LUENDGREN, 9
MACDOWELL, 7
MAGUIRE, 7
MAGUIRE. See also McGUIRE
MALLONEY, 13
MALTMAN, 7
MARDON, 4

MARIE, 4
MARKHAM, 4
MARLOW, 4
MARSDEN, 4
MARTAIN, 4
MARTIN, 4
MATHEWS, 9
MAUSDEN, 4
MAWHENY, 4
McALEER, 13
McALIER, 13
McBRYAN, 13
McCALLEY, 13
McCALLUM, 7
McCASH, 4
McCAWLEY, 13
McCONKEY, 4
McCONNEL, 9
McCREA, 4
McDONALD, 4, 13
McDONALD. See also DONALD
McDONAUGH, 13
McDONOGH, 13
McDOULE, 13
McDOULL, 13
McDOWELL. See MACDOWELL
McEUIN, 4
McGAW, 4
McGEE, 4
McGILL, 9
McGRATH, 4
McGUIRE, 9
McGUIRE. see also MAGUIRE
McKENZIE, 4

McLEOD, 4	NOONAN, 4	REED, 10	SELIG, 8
McLOUGHLIN, 7	NOONON, 4	REEDA, 14	SELIG. See SILLIGH
McMULLAN, 13	NUTT, 4	REEDER, 10	SELWOOD, 5
McMULLEN, 13	O'NEAL, 13	REID, 7	SEXTER, 5
McNAMEE, 13	O'NEIL, 13	REIDA, 14	SEXTON, 5
McPHARSON, 13	O'NEILL, 13	REILY, 4	SHANNON, 10
McPHERSON, 4, 13	OLKERS, 8, 10	REPKEY, 4	SHEELER, 8, 10
McWILLIAMS, 9	ORBINSON. See ORBISON	RICHARDS, 10	SIDAWAY, 5
MELLON, 4	ORBISON, 13	RICHISON, 4	SILLIGH, 8, 10
MERDYTH, 4	ORMAND, 4	RIDLEY, 4	SILWOOD. See SELWOOD
MERIDIETH, 4	ORMON, 4	RIELY, 4	SINCLAIR, 5
MERRITT, 4	ORMOND, 4	RIELY. See REILY	SIXTON, 5
MILLEGAN, 4	OTT, 10	RILEY, 4	SMITH, 5, 10, 14
MITCHELL, 4	PARKE, 4	RILEY. See also REILY	SMYTH, 14
MONAGHAN, 9	PATTERSON, 4	RING, 5	SNELLOCK, 10
MOORE, 4, 13	PENNON, 13	RIPKEY, 4	SNOW, 7
MORGAN, 10, 13	PEPPER, 7	RIPLEY, 4	SOON, 5
MORRISON, 4	PETREKEN, 7	ROACH, 7	SPENCER, 5
MORROUGH, 13	PETREKIN, 7	ROBINSON, 5, 14	STANEFORD, 5
MORTON, 10	PHILIPS, 7	ROHRMANN, 5	STANLEY, 10
MOYLIN, 7	PHILLIPS, 7	ROHRMANN. See also ROMAN	STEINMANN, 8, 10
MULHALL, 4	PICKARD, 4	ROLLINS, 5	STEIR, 5
MULLHOLAND, 13	PIERCE, 10	ROMAN, 5	STEVENS, 5
MULREMAN, 10	PIEROTT, 10	ROMAN. See also ROHRMANN	STIMSON, 5
MULTMAN, 7	POTTER, 4	ROSS, 7, 14	STINEMAN, 8, 10
MULTMAN. See also MALTMAN	PRATT, 4	ROWLINS, 5	STRAHAN, 10
	PRESCOTT, 7	RUEPKE. See REPKEY	STROUS, 7
MURDOCH, 4	PRETZLOW, 4	SANTON, 7	SUMMERS, 14
MURDOCK, 4	PRICE, 13	SAPLE, 10	SUTHERLAND, 5
MURPHEY, 13	PRITCHLER, 4	SAPPLE, 10	SWANTZ, 8, 10
MURPHY, 10, 13	PROCTOR, 10	SCHUELER, 8	TAYLOR, 5, 14
MURRAY, 4, 7	PURDY, 4	SCHUELER. See SHEELER	TEDFORD, 5
NASH, 10	QUIGLEY, 10	SCHWANTZ, 8	THAY, 13
NELSON, 4, 13	QUINN, 14	SCHWANTZ. See SWANTZ	THEIL, 5
NEWBERY, 7	RAWLINS, 4	SCOTT, 5	THOMAS, 10
NEWLANDS, 10	RAY, 14	SEIDEN. See LEIDEN	THOMPSON, 5, 10

ULBRECHT, 8, 10
ULBRIGHT, 8, 10
UPEAN, 5
USS, 8, 10
VEIT, 8, 9
WADMAN, 10
WAID, 5
WALSH, 7, 14
WARD, 5

WARR, 5
WARREN, 5
WATKINS, 7
WEIMAR, 8, 10
WELSHMAN, 10
WEST, 14
WESTON, 5
WETWORTH, 5
WEYMER, 8, 10

WHITAKER, 7
WHITE, 5, 14
WILKINSON, 5, 10
WILKS, 5
WILLIAMS, 5, 10
WILLIS, 5, 10
WILLSON, 10
WILSON, 10
WINEGAR, 8, 10

WINNEGAR, 10
WINTERBOTTOM, 5
WISE, 5
WITWORTH, 5
WITWORTH. See WETWORTH
WOLDEN, 7
WOODS, 5, 14
WRIGHT, 5, 14
YOUNG, 5
ZIERECK, 10

British-American Genealogical Research
Monograph Number 10

DESERTERS AND DISBANDED SOLDIERS FROM BRITISH, GERMAN, AND LOYALIST MILITARY UNITS IN THE SOUTH, 1782

CLIFFORD NEAL SMITH

First Printing, September 1991   uz
Reprint, November 1994   u

INTRODUCTION

This monograph is a transcription of a register in the archives of Fordham University, New York. It accompanies an orderly book of General Nathanael Greene, an American general of the American Revolution. The register is microfilmed in roll 0017787 available from the Family History Center, Salt Lake City, where it is somewhat inexactly catalogued as a "Register of British Deserters ... 7 February 1782 to 16 December 1782."

In fact, only a small portion of the men listed herein were British--at least in the sense that they were brought to America simply to fight and not to settle in the country--and less than half were deserters--if one means they defected from intact fighting corps. The fall of Yorktown on 19 October 1781 is generally held to be the end of the War of Independence; all the men listed in the register defected months thereafter. So, in fact, most of them were simply American stragglers from Loyalist troop units in rapid stages of decomposition and disorganization; most were only trying to get home to wherever they had lived immediately prior to mobilization, or returning to family life. This appears to be especially true of men who got passes to the Carolinas, areas which were widely Loyalist in sympathy from the beginning of the War. Other men, knowing that their Loyalist leanings would subject them to persecution if they returned to former homes in independence-minded neighborhoods (usually in the northern states), struck out for the backwoods or for states where their sympathies were unknown. In the case of the Germans herein, real deserters it must be admitted, they usually headed for Pennsylvania, where there was safety and anonymity among the many German speakers who had settled there before the War.

With exception of men in the British regular regiments and the Hessian mercenary troops, it appears that most men listed hereinafter arrived in the colonies before the outbreak of the War. Even though they listed their original birth countries in the register, the fact that they got passes to rather precise destinations seems to indicate that they already had made settlement in the colonies before the War.

***

Analysis of the register shows something of the difficulty of our current condition in Genealogy. Herein, we have been able to identify some eighty German soldiers in Hessian muster rolls preserved in Marburg and available in the four volumes of computer runs, entitled Hessische Truppen im amerikanischen Unabhaengigkeitskrieg (Hetrina) [Hessian Troops in the American War of Independence]. Veroeffentlichungen der Archivschule Marburg, Institut fuer Archivwissenschaft, Number 10 (Marburg, Germany: The Archives, 1972-1976). This publication is commonly known by its short title "Hetrina" and will be so cited in this monograph with volume and computer entry noted.

Unfortunately, we cannot make such identification of soldiers from regular British regiments, because their muster rolls, with some exceptions, are not available in this country. These muster rolls, in their thousands, are beautifully bound in chronological order in a corpus of manuscripts known as War Office 12 in the Public Record Office, London. The muster rolls of only a very few regiments have been analyzed for desertions, for which see Clifford Neal Smith, British and German Deserters, Dischargees, and Prisoners of War Who May Have Remained in Canada and the United States, 1774-1783. British-American Genealogical research Monograph 9, parts 1 and 2 (McNeal, AZ: Westland Publications, 1988, 1989). Thus, the major task of analyzing the rolls of British troop units which were in America remains to be done. One should add, however, that, RESEARCHERS FINDING A NAME OF INTEREST IN THIS REGISTER, SHOULD CONSULT BRITISH PERSONNEL RECORDS which are available from the Family History Center, Salt Lake City, for which see their card catalog:

> Great Britain, Military Records. War Office. Soldiers' documents ... containing particulars of age, birthplace, etc. [Roll numbers are provided below and designated LDS microfilm].
>
> Great Britain, Military Records, 1789-1820. Muster rolls [of Loyalist troop units in America].

Even worse, the records of American residents of Loyalist sympathy are elusive and hardly accessible, when they exist at all. Nowhere have the been systematically analyzed (some microfilm rolls listed below, however). The prejudice against Loyalists in post-war America was considerable, and their records, such as they are, have been ignored. The militia, whether of Independence or Loyalist persuasion, "were an extremely uncertain element, both to friend and foe," as J. W. Fortescue observed in his thirteen-volume History of the British Army (London: MacMillan, 1899), 3:407. And, as General Washington wrote in his Works, 7:467, regarding even the independence-minded irregular units: "The collecting of the militia depends entirely on the prospects of the day; if favourable, they throng to you; if, not, they will not move."

Researchers finding soldiers of interest to them will want to consult Mark M. Boatner III, Encyclopedia of the American Revolution (New York: David McKay Co., 1966) for a quick overview of the Southern Campaign. This work will be cited as Boatner in this monograph. Thereafter, researchers should consult the many works therein cited for further details on their subjects' probable history.

***

We close this Introduction with short notes on each troop unit. Since defecters often took flight in small groups, and were likely to have found refuge or settled near each other, researchers should keep this in mind when searching for them on the 1790 and 1800 federal decennial censuses of the United States. Hereinafter are the destinations of defecters from each troop unit, plus the individual register entries where their names appear.

BRITISH REGIMENTS OF FOOT

Third British Regiment* (the "Buffs" or East Kent Regiment)
Albany, New York: Entry 004
North Carolina: Entry 288, 289
The regiment was sent out from England to reinforce Clinton and reached Charleston on 17 June 1781 (Fortescue, 3:388). [Defecters are, there-

fore, most likely not to have been previous settlers in America.]
See LDS microfilm rolls 0864767-0864777 for individual personnel records.
*Mentioned in Boatner, p. 1031.

Seventh British Regiment* (the Royal Fusiliers)
North Carolina: Entry 107?
Virginia: Entry 184?
The regiment was already in Canada in 1775. Fortescue says that it was one of only two regiments defending Canada and that it was considered very weak (see Fortescue, 3:155). It was in Clinton's flotilla which arrived in Charleston in January 1780, (Ibid., 3:313 ff).
See LDS microfilm rolls 0864806-0864812 for individual personnel records.
*Mentioned in Boatner, p. 206.

19th British Regiment (the Yorkshire Regiment)
North Carolina, Hillsboro [Hillsborough]: Entry 315
Pennsylvania: Entry 010, 011, 012
The regiment was sent out from England to reinforce Clinton and arrived at Charleston on 17 June 1781 (Fortescue, 3:388 ff). [Therefore, defecters from the regiment are not likely to have been previous settlers in America.]
See LDS microfilm rolls 0876941-0876947 for individual personnel records.

22nd British Regiment (the Cheshire Regiment)
Country [unspecified destination]: Entry 338
Pennsylvania: Entry 062, 063
The regiment fought at Bunker's Hill (17 June 1775) and Brooklyn (22 August 1776) (Fortescue, pp. 161, 184). [There is no further mention of the regiment in Fortescue and it is not known when it was deployed in the Carolinas.]
See LDS microfilm rolls 0872372-087380 for individual personnel records.

23rd British Regiment (the Royal Welsh Fusiliers)*
Pennsylvania: Entry 139, 140
Philadelphia: Entry 204, 205
The regiment fought at Bunker's Hill (17 June 1775) and Brooklyn (22 August 1776) (see Fortescue, 3:161, 184). It was in the flotilla under Clinton which arrived in Charleston in January 1780 (Ibid., 3:313).
See LDS microfilm rolls 0872381-0872388 for individual personnel records.
*Mentioned in Boatner, p. 206

30th British Regiment (First Battalion, East Lancashire Regiment)
Pennsylvania: Entry 921
Philadelphia: Entry 053
The regiment was sent out from England to reinforce Clinton and arrived at Charleston on 17 June 1781 (see Fortescue, 3:388 ff).
See LDS microfilm rolls 0885406-0885411 and 0886552-0886555 for individual personnel records.

33rd British Regiment (First Battalion, West Riding Regiment)*
North Carolina, Camden: Entry 276, 327, 328, 329
North Carolina: Entry 047
Philadelphia: Entry 039, 050, 057
Pennsylvania: Entry 070, 071, 138
Virginia: Entry 282, 283
The regiment fought at the battle of Brandywine Creek in September 1777. It was in Clinton's flotilla which arrived in Charleston in January 1780 (see Fortescue, 3:215 and 313 ff).
See LDS microfilm rolls 0885431-0885436 for individual personnel records.
*Mentioned in Boatner, pp. 206, 210.

60th British Regiment (King's Royal Rifle Corps)*
Charleston [SC]: Entry 343, 344
Country [unspecified destination]: Entry 334, 337, 346, 348, 349
Dutch Fork? [unidentified location]: Entry 331, 333
North Carolina: Entry, 082, 339, 340?, 345, 351
Pennsylvania: Entry 341, 342, 352
South Carolina: Entry 340?
Virginia: Entry 353
In 1763 the regiment formed the garrisons of outposts in the Old Northwest Territory (Sault St. Marie, Fort Pitt, Fort Ligonier, Presquile, and Niagara, among others) "composed in great measure of foreigners both officers and men" (see Fortescue, 3:13). Its augmentation in 1775 was again mainly foreign (Ibid., 3:173). Four hundred sickly men of the regiment surrendered to the French fleet at St. Vincent Island in the Carribean in June 1779 (Ibid, 3:273).
See LDS microfilm rolls 0898121-0898142 for individual personnel records.
*Mentioned in Boatner, p. 986.

63rd British Regiment (First Battalion, Manchester Regiment)*
North Carolina, Georgetown: Entry 247
Philadelphia: Entry 203
Virginia: Entry 296
The regiment arrived in New York in July 1776 (Fortescue, 3:184), and was in Clinton's flotilla which landed at Charleston in January 1780 (Ibid., 3:313 ff).
See LDS microfilm rolls 0898156-0898166 for individual personnel records.
*Mentioned in Boatner, p. 206.

64th British Regiment (First Battalion, North Staffordshire Regiment)*
Country [unspecified location]: Entry 347
This regiment arrived in New York in July 1776 (Fortescue, 3:184) and was in Clinton's flotilla which landed at Charleston in January 1780 (Ibid., 3:313 ff).
See LDS microfilm rolls 0898166-0898174 for individual personnel records.
*Mentioned in Boatner, pp. 206, 210.

71st British Regiment (same as Fraser's Highlanders below)*
Delaware?, Wilmington: Entry 183
North Carolina?, Wilmington: Entry 183
North Carolina: Entry 107?, 350
Pennsylvania: Entry 221, 244, 269, 270
Virginia: Entry 184
The regiment was organized in 1775 (Fortescue, 3:175); its correct title was the 71st Highland Light Infantry; one infers that the original recruits were from Scotland (Ibid, 3:247). By July 1776 it was in New York (Ibid., 3:184).

See LDS microfilm rolls 0898326-0898334 for individual personnel records.
*Mentioned in Boatner, pp. 206, 208, 397-398, 1062.

82d British Regiment (Francis M'Lean's Regiment)*
Pennsylvania: Entry 243
Philadelphia: Entry 113, 114, 185
First organized in the spring of 1778 (Fortescue, 3:247 ff); apparently recruits were from Scotland.
See LDS microfilm rolls 0903623-0903631 for individual personnel records.
*Mentioned in Boatner, p. 1038.

84th British Regiment (Royal Highland Emigrants, or Allan Maclean's Regiment)*
Pennsylvania: Entry 197
Fortescue states that "a very capable officer", Colonel Allan Maclean had assembled nearly 400 recruits in Sorel, Canada, in 1775, when he heard that Arnold had appeared before Quebec. Maclean then made a forced march to the city, reaching it on 13 November 1775. Thus, it would appear that most recruits for this Regiment were Scotch settlers from the Sorel area. (see Fortescue, 3:165).
See LDS microfilm rolls 0904039-0904050 for individual personnel records.
*Mentioned in Boatner, p. 1038.

[Illegible] British Regiment
Pennsylvania: Entry 078
North Carolina: Entry 079

OTHER BRITISH UNITS

First Regular Guards
Pennsylvania: Entry 136
Philadelphia: Entry 022

Third Regular Guards
Philadelphia: Entry 023, 072

Fifth Regular Guards
Philadelphia: Entry 091, 092, 093

Brown's or Browne's Corps* (also known as the Prince of Wales Loyal American Volunteers, which see herein)
Broad River: Entry 202
North Carolina, Georgetown: Entry 310
Virginia: Entry 081
[Destination not given] Entry 201
See LDS microfilm rolls 0928945-0928946 for individual personnel records.
See article entitled "Prince of Wales Loyal American Volunteers" in Boatner, p. 890.
*Mentioned in Ibid., p. 210.

Fanning's Regiment* (also known as the Associated Refugees or the King's American Regiment of Foot, which see herein)
New York: Entry 220
New York State: Entry 233
Pennsylvania: 083
A provincial corps raised in New York in 1776 (Fortescue, 3:386 ff).
See LDS microfilm roll 0928946 for individual personnel records.
*See article entitled "Fanning's Regiment" in Boatner, p. 362; also mentioned in Ibid., pp. 1032, 1038.

Fraser Highlanders (same as 71st British Regiment above)
Broad River: Entry 097, 174, 175, 176, 178, 254, 264,
Broad & Salada Rivers: Entry 224, 225, 226, 227
Congaree [River]: Entry 094
Ninety-Six District [South Carolina]: Entry 056, 167, 169, 170, 218, 232, 248
North Carolina: Entry 088, 089, 090, 177, 215, 249, 250, 251, 252, 253, 255, 265
Virginia: Entry 217, 219, 258, 259, 260
[Illegible Destination]: Entry 126
Two battalions of this unit, also known as the 71st British Regiment, were in the expedition from New York that captured Savannah on 29 December 1778. Presumably, most of the original soldiers were recruited in Great Britain, mainly Scotland, arriving in America in 1776, but it is possible that they were supplemented by local Loyalists recruited in America.
See LDS microfilm rolls 0898326-0898334 for individual personnel records.
See article entitled "Fraser Highlanders" in Boatner, pp. 397-398.

King's American Regiment (also known as Fanning's Regiment and the Associated Refugees, which see herein)
New England: Entry 297
Philadelphia: 281
The regiment was a provincial corps raised by Colonel Fanning in New York in 1776 (Fortescue, 3:386 ff.
See LDS microfilm roll 0928946 for individual personnel records.

King's Rangers* (also known as the South Carolina King's Rangers, commanded by Colonel Thomas Brown)
Georgia, Augusta: Entry 188, 189
New York State: Entry 241
Pennsylvania: Entry 127
Philadelphia: Entry 156, 157
South Carolina, Tiger River**: Entry 187
Virginia: Entry 186
See LDS microfilm rolls 0928945-0928946 for individual personnel records.
*See Boatner, pp. 890, 1031.
**A "little skirmish" damaging to the British, because it "interrupted the sequence, hitherto unbroken, of Tarleton's successes" (Fortescue, 3:363).

Lord Rawdon's Corps*
North Carolina: Entry 223
Pennsylvania: Entry 103
Philadelphia: 098, 099, 100
*See Boatner, p. 210.
Note that a number of troop units came to the Carolinas from New York under Lord Rawdon, later the Marquess of Hastings, and could be referred to as "Rawdon's Corps." One corps, known as the Volunteers of Ireland, was composed "entirely of

Irish deserters from the American army under the colonelcy of Lord Rawdon" (see Fortescue, 3:276, 386).
See LDS microfilm roll 0928945 for individual personnel records of the Volunteers of Ireland.

Prince of Wales Loyal American Volunteers*, (also called Brown's Regiment, which see herein)
Connecticut: Entry 095, 271
Maryland: Entry 195
[New?] Jersey: Entry 096
New York: Entry 273
New York State: Entry 111, 112
North Carolina: Entry 027, 196, 266, 267, 268
Pennsylvania: Entry 024
Philadelphia: Entry 212
Rhode Island: Entry 026
See LDS microfilm rolls 0928945-0928946 for individual personnel records.
*See article entitled "Prince of Wales Loyal American Volunteers" in Boatner, p. 890; see also mention of this unit in Ibid., p. 210.

Refugee Corps (also known as Fanning's Regiment and the King's American Regiment, which see herein)
Broad River: Entry 106
Destination not stated: 061
See LDS microfilm roll 0928946 for individual personnel records.

NAVAL VESSELS AND PRIVATEERS

Adder (Galley)
South Carolina, Georgetown: Entry 080

Ajourande [possibly the Adeljunde Luise*]
Philadelphia: Entry 130, 131
South Carolina, Georgetown: Entry 122, 123, 124, 125
*Mentioned in Hetrina, 3:0018, as a transport ship for Hessian Garrison Regiment von Wissenbach, later von Knoblauch.

Bellesarico
Pennsylvania: Entry 324
Rhode Island: Entry 325

Farley (transport ship)
Pennsylvania: Entry 216

Fire Fly (ship)
Pennsylvania: Entry 087

Greyhound (ship?)
South Carolina, Georgetown: Entry 318, 319, 320
South Carolina: Entry 321

Holder (galley)
Maryland, Ligonier*: Entry 019, 020
*There is a Ligonier, Pennsylvania.

Lark (galley)
Philadelphia: Entry 286, 287

Lovely Cass (ship?)
South Carolina, Georgetown: Entry 155

Rattle Snake (ship)
Philadelphia: Entry 115

Scorpion (galley)
Philadelphia: Entry 076

Trimmer (galley)
Philadelphia: Entry 234

Viper (galley)
Pennsylvania: Entry 008, 009, 073, 074
Philadelphia: Entry 137

Vulture (sloop of war)
Maryland: Entry 242

[Illegible ships and galley]
Philadelphia: 116, 117, 118, 330

ASSOCIATED GERMAN (HESSIAN) CORPS

Feldjaeger [Detachment]*
Pennsylvania: Entry 042
*Mentioned in Boatner, pp. 206, 208, 549.
*According to Hetrina, 4:0011, the Feldjaeger-Korps was made up entirely of volunteers, unlike other Hessian units. Volunteers were admitted only after testing as sharpshooters, and most of them had been hunters in civil life. Jaeger companies were organized at various times, after it was found that the sharpshooters were particularly effective in America. Detachments of Feldjaegern were active in nearly all the battles, including Trenton, Brandywine Creek, Redbank, Fort Constitution, Charleston, Springfield, and Philipps House. The Corps left New York for Europe in November 1783.

Regiment von Angelelli*
Pennsylvania: Entry 144, 147, 148, 208, 213
Philadelphia: Entry 152, 153, 154
Virginia: Entry 121, 308, 309
*According to Hetrina, 3:0016, this regiment, originally designated Regiment von Rall, arrived in America in August 1776 and was stationed on Staten Island, New York. It took part in actions at White Plains, Fort Washington, Fort Lee, Trenton, Brandywine Creek, and the occupation of Philadelphia. After transfer of command to the Marquis d'Angelelli (also spelled Angelelly), it was sent to the Carolinas, as part of the British expeditionary force, and took part at the action at Stono Ferry (James Island, east of Charleston) and Savannah. The British evacuated Savannah on 11 July 1782 and Charleston on 14 December 1782, and Regiment von Angelelli was transported back to Europe beginning on 14 August 1783.

Regiment von Benning*
Camden [probably North Carolina]: Entry 277, 278
Pennsylvania: Entry 065, 066, 068, 069, 141, 142,

145, 150
Stono [probably Stono Ferry, James Island, South Carolina]: Entry 284, 285, 294, 295
According to Hetrina, 1:0013, this regiment was originally designated the Garrison Regiment von Huyn. It arrived in America at the end of October 1776 and was militarily active thereafter in New York and New Jersey; later at Brandywine Creek, Germantown, and Redbank. At the end of 1779, newly designated the Garrison Regiment von Benning, it was transported to the Carolinas, arriving in February 1780 and returned from Charleston to Long Island in the winter of 1782-1783. In August 1783 the regiment was returned to Europe.
*See Boatner, pp. 1034-1035, 1062.

Regiment von Ditfurth*
    North Carolina, Camden: Entry 304, 305, 306, 307, 314, 316
    North Carolina: Entry 200
    Pennsylvania: 025, 067, 146, 206, 207, 235, 236, 237, 292, 293
    Virginia: Entry 245
    [Destination not given] Entry 182
    According to Hetrina, 2:0011, this regiment arrived at Staten Island, New York, in August 1776. It took part in battles at Newport and Charleston. After reorganization in 1782 it returned to New York. In August 1783 the regiment was returned to Europe.
    *Mentioned in Boatner, p. 210.

Regiment von Knoblauch
    North Carolina, Camden: Entry 313
    Pennsylvania: Entry 013, 014, 015, 016, 017, 030, 031, 032, 033, 034, 035, 036, 048, 086, 128, 129, 143, 274, 275
    Philadelphia: Entry 048, 051, 052, 101, 102, 166
    Virginia: Entry 246
    According to Hetrina, 3:0018, this unit was originally designated the Garrison Regiment von Wissenbach. It arrived at Sandy Hook, NY, in October 1776, landing at New Rochelle. It went through a number of reorganizations and mergers with other troop units, finally coming under the command of Major General Hans von Knoblauch. In the southern expedition the regiment was under the command of Captain Henger of the Jaegerkorps and took part in the siege of Savannah and the affair at Gibbshouse.

STATE MILITIA CORPS

De Lancy's Corps, (also known as the New York Volunteer Corps, which see herein)
    Connecticut: Entry 262, 263
    North Carolina: Entry 317
    See LDS microfilm rolls 0928943-0928944 for individual personnel records.

Georgia Loyalists*
    Pennsylvania, York County: Entry 006, 007
    Virginia: Entry 005
    *Mentioned in Boatner, p. 1031.

First Maryland Regiment
    To go hunting: Entry 501

Fought well at Guilford Court House, 15 March 1781; estimated to have about 285 men (Fortescue, 3:379, 380 ff).
See LDS microfilm rolls 0928946-0928947 for individual personnel records.

New York Volunteer Corps (also called De Lancy's Corps, for which see herein)*
    Maryland: Entry 272
    Massachusetts, Boston: Entry 290
    New York, Albany: 291
    New York: Entry 198, 199
    New York State: Entry 108, 158, 159, 160, 161, 162, 163, 298, 299, 302, 303, 311, 312
    North Carolina, Camden: Entry 300
    North Carolina: Entry 110
    Pennsylvania: Entry 077, 109, 149
    Philadelphia: Entry 049, 075, 301
    South Carolina: Entry 279, 280,
    See LDS microfilm rools 0928943-0928944 for individual personnel records.
    *Mentioned in Boatner, pp. 206 ff, 802.

First North Carolina Regiment
    To go hunting: Entry 502

Second North Carolina Regiment
    To go hunting: Entry 503

North Carolina Highlanders (also known as George Martin's Corps, which see below)
    Guilford [Court House], North Carolina: Entry 001, 002, 003
    North Carolina: Entry 028, 029, 044, 045, 54, 055, 172, 173, 209, 210, 211
    Maryland: Entry 018?, 240

George Martin's Corps (also known as the North Carolina Highlanders, which see above)
    North Carolina: Entry 172, 173, 209, 210, 211
    South Carolina: Entry 151
    [No destinatin given] Entry 171

North Carolina Independent Troops
    North Carolina: Entry 040, 041

North Carolina Loyalists
    Broad River: Entry 046
    North Carolina: Entry 060, 256, 257
    Virginia: Entry 261

North Carolina Royalists (also called Colonel Hamilton's Regiment*)
    North Carolina: Entry 119, 228, 229, 230, 231
    Philadelphia: Entry 238, 239
    South Carolina, Orangeburg: Entry 192, 193, 194
    Virginia: Entry 222
    *Mentioned in Boatner, pp. 208-209.

South Carolina Loyalists*
    North Carolina: Entry 335, 336
    South Carolina: Entry 064
    *Probably the unit called the South Carolina Royalists, under [Colonel?] Innes, Boatner p.208
    See LDS microfilm roll 0928946 for individual personnel records.

UNIDENTIFIED TROOP UNITS

<u>Artificers</u>
    Destination not given: Entry 168

<u>Captain Gilles' Regiment</u>
    North Carolina: Entry 120

<u>Colonel Bevan's Unit</u>
    Broad River: Entry 179
    Georgia, Augusta: Entry 180, 181

<u>Dragoons</u>
    Pennsylvania: Entry 104, 105
    There were several dragoon units in America by 1776 (Fortescue, 3:175).

<u>Duke of Cumberland Regiment</u>
    Maryland: Entry 323
    Virginia: Entry 322
    Assuredly not a regiment in the British regular establishment because not listed in Fortescue.

<u>Lieutenant Colonel Merritt's Corps</u>
    Maryland: Entry 191
    South Carolina, Camden: 190

FORMAT OF ENTRIES

The entries are sequentially numbered in the original register and so appear in this monograph.

The first line of each entry gives the date and place of defection.

The second line gives the name, country of origin, and craft. This data is not in the order in which it appears in the original register.

The third line gives the name of the troop unit from which the individual defected.

The fourth line gives the destination for which the individual was given a pass by American officers.

001 1782 February 04, Quarterhouse
McDONALD, Archibald, Corporal, born in Scotland, laborer
North Carolina Highlanders, [officer] G. Martin
Pass to Guilford, North Carolina

002 1782 February 04, Quarterhouse
PATTERSON, Daniel, Corporal, born in North Carolina, laborer
North Carolina Highlanders, [officer] G. Martin
Pass to Guilford, North Carolina

003 1782 February 04, Quarterhouse
McCRAE, Chris[tophe]r, private, born in Scotland, laborer
North Carolina Highlanders, [officer] G. Martin
Pass to Guilford, North Carolina

004 1782 February 04, Quarterhouse
McQUIN, John, private, born in Scotland, weaver
3rd British Regiment
Pass to Albany, New York
Research Note: There appear to be no extant muster rolls dating from the 1781-1782 period in Public Records Office, War Office 12, volume 2105. See Clifford Neal Smith, British and German Deserters, Dischargees, and Prisoners of War Who May Have Remained in Canada and the United States, 1774-1783. British-American Genealogical Research Monograph Number 9, Part 2 (McNeal, AZ: Westland Publications, 1989), pp. 11-12.

005 1782 February 06, Gursbach? in Savannah River
BURRELL, George, Corporal, born in England, carpenter
Georgia Loyalists
Pass to Virginia

006 1782 February 06, Gursbach? in Savannah River
SPENCER, Edward, private, born in England, blacksmith
Georgia Loyalists
Pass to York County, Pennsylvania

007 1782 February 00?, Gursbach? in Savannah River
GAYIMAN?, Christopher?, private, born in Germany, laborer
Georgia Loyalists
Pass to York County, Pennsylvania

008 1782 February 03, Viper Galley at New Cul--?
MANURE, David, born in Ireland, sailor
[Viper Galley]
Pass to Pennsylvania

009 1782 February 03, Viper Galley
MARIOT, Thomas, born in the West Indies, sailor
[Viper Galley]
Pass to Pennsylvania

010 1782 February 04, Quarterhouse
HETSWORTH, John, born in England, tailor
19th British Regiment
Pass to Pennsylvania

011 1782 February 04, Quarterhouse
LENDON?/SENDON?, Pat[rick], born in Ireland, laborer
19th British Regiment
Pass to Pennsylvania

012 1782 February 04, Quarterhouse
ACHKINS, Robert, born in England, laborer
19th British Regiment
Pass to Pennsylvania

013 1782 February 10, Savannah
CROUS, John, a Hessian, laborer
Regiment von Knoblauch
Pass to Pennsylvania
Research Note: (a) According to Hetrina, 3:3410, soldier KRAUSS/GRAUSS, Johannes, born 1757-1758, from Moegen?/Meden?/Metter?, deserted in February 1782 from the second company of Garrison Regiment von Wissenbach, later von Knoblauch.
(b) A village named Moegen in Dresden Regierungsbezirk in East Germany, coordinates: 51-11N 13-13E; a stream called the Metter in Baden-Wuerttemberg, cordinates: 48-58N 9-08E.

014 1782 February 10, Savannah
CLINE, Philip, a Hessian, laborer
Regiment von Knoblauch
Pass to Pennsylvania
Research Notes: (a) According to Hetrina 2:3546, soldier KLEIN/GLEIN, Philipp, born 1761-1762, from Rauschenberg, Hessen, deserted in February 1782 from the second company of Garrison Regiment von Wissenbach, later von Knoblauch.
(b) There are several villages named Rauschenberg in West Germany.
(c) According to 1871 Prussian census, Rauschenberg, Hessen, in Hessen-Nassau, Regierungsbezirk Kassel, Kreis Kirchhain, Stadtgemeinde Rauschenberg, had a total population of 1298 (1231 protestants, 17 Catholics, 50 Jews); thus presumably an Evangelical Lutheran church in Rauschenberg.
(d) Geographic coordinates for Rauschenberg, Hessen: 50-53N 8-55E.
(e) Preliminary Survey (1979) reports that Family History Center, Salt Lake City, has 16 rolls of microfilm from Justizamt [court] from Rauschenberg, 1783-1874.

015 1782 February 10, Savannah
SMITH, John, a Hessian, laborer
Regiment von Knoblauch
Pass to Pennsylvania
Research Note: (a) According to Hetrina 3:1313 soldier SCHMIDT, Johannes, born 1754-1775, from Dietzbach, Silesia, or Doerzbach, deserted February 1782 from company 3 Garrison Regiment von Wissenbach, later von Knoblauch.
(b) There is a village of Doerzbach in Oberfranken, Baden-Wuerttemberg; coordinates: 49-23N 9-42E.
(c) According to Preliminary Survey (1979) the Family History Center, Salt Lake City, has a microfilm roll of the Evangelical church records of Doerzbach, 1596-1835.

016 1782 February 10, Savannah
WERNER?/WERSEN?, John, a Hessian, laborer
Regiment von Knoblauch
Pass to Pennsylvania
Research Note: According to Hetrina 3:15860, soldier WERNER, Johann Jakob, no birth date or place, was transferred into Regiment von Rall in December 1776; under arrest from March 1779 to July 1781; dismissed from army August 1781 [although this identification is doubtful, it might have been that he was subsequently drafted in Garrison Regiment von Wissenbach, later von Knoblauch, but not reported in any muster roll].

017 1782 February 10, Savannah
WALPOLER?/WALPOLEN?, William, a Hessian, laborer
Regiment von Knoblauch
Pass to Pennsylvania
Research Note: (a) According to Hetrina 3:15511, soldier WALPER, Wilhelm, born 1757-1758, from Schwarzenhasel, Hessen, deserted from the fifth company of Garrison Regiment von Wissenbach, later von Knoblauch, in February 1782.
(b) According to 1871 Prussian census, Hessen-Nassau, Regierungsbezirk Kassel, Kreis Rotenberg an der Fulda, Landgemeinde Schwartzenhasel, had a total population of 412, all protestants.
(c) Geographic coordinates 51-01N 9-46E.
(d) According to Preliminary Survey, the Family History Center, Salt Lake City, has two rolls of microfilm from the Justizamt Schwarzenhasel [court records], 1815-1875.

018 1782 February 18, Quarterhouse
ENNIS?/EUTUS?, Daniel, born in Ireland, cooper
North Carolina Hussars?/Highlanders?
Pass to Maryland

019 1782 February 25, Holder? Galley at the Cab--?
FINNIS?/TINNIS?, Drury?, from France, no occupation given [probably a sailor]
[Holder? Galley]
Pass to Maryland, Ligonier?

020 1782 February 25, Holder? Galley at the Cab--?
GASPEE?/GASPER?, David?, from France, no occupation given [probably a sailor]
[Holder Galley]
Pass to Maryland, Ligonier?
Research Note: According to Hetrina 3:5723 GASPER, Henrich, no birth year, from Nordhausen, died aboard ship in January 1782. He had been in company 5 of Garrison Regiment von Wissenbach, later von Knoblauch. This identification seems doubtful.

021 1782 February 27, Quarterhouse
OWENS, Terence, from Ireland, weaver
30th British Regiment
Pass to Pennsylvania

022 1782 March 04, James Island
CATON, Thomas?, from England, carpenter
First Regiment Guards
Pass to Philadelphia

023 1782 March 04, James Island
LINSLEY, William, from Scotland, carpenter
Third Regiment Guards
Pass to Philadelphia

024 1782 March 04, James Island
BENDER, Matthias, from Germany, forgeman
Prince of Wales Regiment
Pass to Pennsylvania

025 1782 March 04, James Island
MILLER, Henry, from Germany, baker
Von Ditfurth Regiment
Pass to Pennsylvania
Research Notes: (a) According to Hetrina 2:7239, soldier MUELLER, Johann Henrich, no birth date, from Weilmuenster, Hessen, deserted in March 1782 from the first company of Regiment von Ditfurth. (There were other deserters of this name, for which see Hetrina 2:7026, 2:7028, 2:7209, 3:10013, but none from Regiment von Ditfurth.)
(b) According to the Prussian census of 1871, Hessen-Nassau, Regierungsbezirk Wiesbaden, Oberlahnkreis, Flecken [market town] Weilmuenster, had a total population of 1458 (1395 Protestants, 32 Catholics, 31 Jews)
(c) Geographic coordinates: 50-24N 8-27E.

026 1782 March 06, James Island
PAINE, Edward, American from Rhode Island, farmer
Prince of Wales Regiment
Pass to Rhode Island

027 1782 March 07, James Island
SAMPSON, William, from Ireland, blacksmith
Prince of Wales Regiment
Pass to North Carolina

028 1782 March 07, Quarterhouse
STEWARD, John, Sr.?, from Scotland, farmer
North Carolina Highlanders
Pass to North Carolina

029 1782 March 07, Quarterhouse
McCLOUSS?, Peter, from Scotland, farmer
North Carolina Highlanders
Pass to North Carolina

030 1782 March 02, Savannah
MERLS?/MERLO?, Peter, from Germany, blacksmith
Regiment von Knoblauch
Pass to Pennsylvania
Research Note: (a) According to Hetrina, 3:9466, soldier MARLO, Peter, born 1756-1757, from Heisterberg/Heisba, deserted in March 1782 from company 5 of Garrison Regiment von Wissenbach, later von Knoblauch.
(b) There are three villages and one farm called Heisterberg in West Germany; two of the villages are in Hessen:
  (i) Hessen-Nassau, Regierungsbezirk Wiesbaden, Dillkreis, Amt Herborn, Landgemeinde Heisterberg, total population 128, all protestant.
  (ii) Not listed in Prussian census.
(c) Geographic coordinates for the two Hessian villages: 50-39N 8-09E and 50-34N 8-29E.

031 1782 March 02, Savannah
HORTER, Adam, from Germany, carpenter
Regiment von Knoblauch
Pass to Pennsylvania
Research Notes: (a) According to Hetrina, 3:7578, soldier HERTER, Adam, born 1756-1757, from Boppard, deserted from first company, Regiment von Wissenbach, later von Knoblauch, in March 1782.
(b) Two villages of this name, both in Rheinland-Pfalz:
   (i) According to the Prussian census of 1871, Hessen-Nassau, Regierungsbezirk Koblenz, Kreis Sankt Goar, Burgermeisterei Stadt Boppard. Total population 4977 (4360 Catholic, 540 Protestant, 76 Jews)
   (ii) Hessen-Nassau, Regierungsbezirk Koblenz, Kreis Sankt Goar, Buergermeisterei Land Boppard. Neighboring churches at Salzig and Nieder-Spay, both Catholic.
(c) Geographic coordinates: 50-05N 7-42E and 50-14N 7-36E.
(d) According to Preliminary Survey, the Family History Center, Salt Lake City, has 8 rolls of microfilm of Catholic and Evangelical church records for Boppard.

032 1782 March 02, Savannah
HENEISEN, Matthias, from Germany, farmer
Regiment von Knoblauch
Pass to Pennsylvania
Research Notes: (a) According to Hetrina, 3:7440, soldier HENEISEN, Matthaeus, born 1755-1757, from Oberesslingen, deserted from first company of Garrison Regiment von Wissenbach, later von Knoblauch, in March 1782.
(b) Geographic coordinates for Oberesslingen, now in Baden-Wuerttemberg: 48-44N 9-20E.
(c) According to Preliminary Survey, the Family History Center, Salt Lake City, has the following:
   (i) Esslingen/Donaueschingen, Catholic church registers from 1595-1900;
   (ii) Esslingen/Esslingen, Catholic church registers from 1695-1900.

033 1782 March 02, Savannah
BRENWALT, Eus[tac]e?, from Germany, shoemaker
Regiment von Knoblauch
Pass to Pennsylvania
Research Notes: (a) According to Hetrina, 3:1705, soldier BRENNEWALT, Jost, born 1751-1752, from Felsberg, Hessen, deserted from company 4 of Garrison Regiment von Wissenbach, later von Knoblauch, in February 1782. [Possibly siblings of Jost Brennewalt, Andreas (born 1762-1763) and Antrecht (born 1760-1761) in Regiment von Rall.]
(b) There are three villages named Felsberg in West Germany, two in Hessen.
(c) According to Prussian census of 1871, Hessen-Nassau, Regierungsbezirk Kassel, Kreis Melsungen, Stadtgemeinde Felsberg. Total population 1026 (848 Protestants, 168 Jews).
(d) According to Preliminary Survey, the Family History Center, Salt Lake City, has microfilms of the Felsberg/Melsungen Amtsgericht [local court] and Standesamt [personal registry] from 1808 to 1884.

034 1782 March 02, Savannah
SHAFFER, John, from Germany, laborer
Regiment von Knoblauch
Pass to Pennsylvania
Research Notes: (a) According to Hetrina, 3:12592 and 3:12596, soldier SCHAEFFER, Johannes, born 1720-1722, from Lauscheid, deserted from the company 4 of Garrison Regiment von Wissenbach, later von Knoblauch, in July 1782; he was arrested after desertion in October 1782; released from arrest and again deserted April 1783. [Identification of this person is not certain, though probable.]
(b) The Prussian census of 1871 does not list a place name Lauscheid. However, it does list Rheinland-Pfalz, Regierungsbezirk Koblenz, Kreis Meisenheim, Landgemeinde Lauschied. Total population 539 (206 Protestants, 329 Catholics).
(c) Geographic coordinates: 49-44N 7-37E
(d) According to Preliminary Survey, the Family History Center, Salt Lake City, has Evangelical and Catholic church records from 1695-1921.

035 1782 March 02, Savannah
MYER, Ad., from Germany, laborer
Regiment von Knoblauch
Pass to Pennsylvania
Research Notes: (a) According to Hetrina, 3:9827, soldier MEYER, Adam, born 1750-1759, from Reinhardshofen or Rennertshofen, deserted from company 2, Garrison Regiment von Wissenbach, later von Knoblauch, in March 1782.
(b) There are four villages named Rengershausen in West Germany, two in Hessen:
   (i) According to Prussian census of 1871, Hessen-Nassau, Regierungsbezirk Kassel, Landkreis Kassel, Landgemeinde Rengershausen. Total population 380 (all Protestant);
   (ii) Hessen-Nassau, Regierungsbezirk Kassel, Kreis Frankenberg, Landgemeinde Rengershausen. Total population 303 (all Protestant);
(c) There are two villages named Rennertshofen, both in Bavaria. Their coordinates are 48-15N 10-14E and 48-45N 11-04E.
(d) According to Preliminary Survey, the Family History Center, Salt Lake City, has Rangershausen* Justizamt [court] records for 1802-1846 and Rennertehausen* Landgemeinde [village] records for 1768-1846, both villages in Hessen.
*So spelled.

036 1782 March 02, Savannah
EDLER, Francis, from Germany, carpenter
Regiment von Knoblauch
Pass to Pennsylvania
Research Notes: (a) Accordingto Hetrina 3:0067, soldier ADLER, Franz, born 1753-1755, from Birgstein/Bohemia, deserted company 2, Garrison Regiment von Wissenbach, later Knoblauch, in March 1782.
(b) Birgstein/Bohemia probably is Burgstein/Bohemia, a farm, at 48-31N 14-35E.

037 1782 March 01 Blanford Galley
HARRIS, Thomas, from Ireland, sailor
[Blanford Galley]
Pass to Virginia

038 1782 March 01, Blanford Galley
    STILL? Peter, from England, sailor
    [Blanford Galley]
    Pass to Virginia

039 1782 March 26, James Island
    KING, James, from Ireland, farmer
    33rd British Regiment
    Pass to Philadelphia

040 1782 March 29, Quarterhouse
    SMITH, William, from North Carolina, farmer
    North Carolina Independent Troops of North Carolinians [officer] Captain Gilles
    Pass to North Carolina

041 1782 March 29, Quarterhouse
    LAMBERT, Uriah, from North Carolina, farmer
    North Carolina Independent Troops of North Carolinians, [officer] Captain Gilles
    Pass to North Carolina

042 1782 March 30, Quarterhouse
    STAFFAN, Ludwig, from Germany, farmer
    Yager [Jaeger Battalion]
    Pass to Pennsylvania
    Research Notes: (a) According to Hetrina, 4:6817, Jaeger [chasseur] STEPHAN, Ludwig, no birthdate, from Bassenheim [area], West Germany, deserted company 4, Feldjaeger-Korps, in April 1782.
    (b) According to Prussian census of 1871, Provinz Rheinland, Regierungsbezirk Koblenz, Kreis Koblenz, Buergermeisterei Bassenheim. Total population 809 (755 Catholics, 6 Protestants, 32 Jews).
    (c) Geographic coordinates: 50-22N 7-28E.
    (d) According to Preliminary Survey, the Family History Center, Salt Lake City, has microfilms of Bassenheim Catholic church records, 1660-1889.

043 1782 April 06, Quarterhouse?
    KENT, John, place of origin not given, farmer
    Military unit not given
    Pass to Camden

044 1782 April 06, Quarterhouse
    SEELY? John, from Scotland, wheelwright
    North Carolina Highlanders
    Pass to North Carolina

045 1782 April 06, Quarterhouse
    McCOY, George, from Scotland, shoemaker
    North Carolina Highlanders
    Pass to North Carolina

046 1782 April 07, Quarterhouse?
    COTTON, Samuel, American, farmer
    South? Carolina Loyalists
    Pass to Broad? River, North Carolina

047 1782 April 10, James Island and Savannah
    McMAHON, Barney, from Ireland, laborer
    33rd British Regiment
    Pass to North Carolina

048 1782 April 10, James Island and Savannah
    FRISELAND, George, from Germany, farmer
    Regiment von Knoblauch
    Pass to Philadelphia
    Research Note: (a) According to Hetrina, 3:5557, soldier FRIESLAND, Johann Georg, born 1756-1757, from Verden, deserted from the first company of Garrison Regiment von Wissenbach, later von Knoblauch, in April 1782.
    (b) According to Prussian census of 1871, Provinz Hannover, Regierungsbezirk Stade, Kreis Verden, Stadtgemeinde Verden. Total population 6838 (6405 Protestant, 295 Catholics, 123 Jews).
    (c) Geographic coordinates: 52-55N 9-14E, now in Niedersachsen, West Germany.
    (d) According to Preliminary Survey, the Family History Center, Salt Lake City, has the Swedish military records from Verden, 1620-1723, and the Evangelical military church register from Verden, 1819-1942.

049 1782 April 05, James Island
    DOBBS, David, American, wheelwright
    New York Volunteers
    Pass to Philadelphia

050 1782 April 10, James Island
    CONNER, William, from Ireland, farmer
    33rd British Regiment
    Pass to Philadelphia

051 1782 April 05, Savannah
    BRUCK? BRUNCK?, Ch[ristia]n?, from Germany, laborer
    Regiment von Knoblauch
    Pass to Philadelphia
    Research Notes: (a) According to Hetrina, 3:1552, soldier BRAKE, Christoph, born 1758-1759, from Vahlbruch, deserted from the first company of Regiment von Wissenbach, later von Knoblauch, in April 1782. [This identification probable.]
    (b) According to the Prussian census of 1871, Provinz Hannover, Kreis Hameln, Amt Polle, Landgemeinde Vahlbruch. Total population 616 (all Protestant).
    (c) Geographic coordinates: 51-55N 9-21E, now in Niedersachsen, West Germany

052 1782 April 05, Savannah
    SHELHURST, John, from Germany, laborer
    Regiment von Knoblauch
    Pass to Philadelphia
    Research Notes: (a) According to Hetrina, 3:12761, soldier SCHELLHASE, Johannes, born 1754-1757, from Messel, deserted from the first company of Garrison Regiment von Wissenbach, later von Knoblauch, in April 1782.
    (b) Messel not listed in the Prussian census of 1871.
    (c) Geographic coordinates: 49-56N 8-45E, now in Hessen, West Germany.
    (d) According to Preliminary Survey, the Family History Center, Salt Lake City, has the Messel Evangelical church register from 1808-1875.

053 1782 April 14, Quarterhouse
   LIDSTER, John, from England, laborer
   30th [British] Regiment
   Pass to Philadelphia

054 1782 April 14, Quarterhouse
   MURPHEY, Barth[olomew], American, farmer
   North Carolina Highlanders
   Pass to North Carolina

055 1782 April --?, Quarterhouse?
   McCLAINE, John, from Scotland, farmer
   North Carolina Highlanders
   Pass to North Carolina

056 1782 April 17, Quarterhouse
   POWELL, Benjamin, from Virginia, farmer
   Major Frazer's Corps
   Pass to Ninety-Six

057 1782 April 17, James Island
   BARNUM, John, Sr.?, from England, weaver
   33rd British Regiment
   Pass to Philadelphia

058 1782 March 17, *Otter*, sloop of war
   STONE, William, Sr.?, from Ireland, sailor
   [*Otter* sloop of war]
   Pass to Philadelphia

059 1782 April --?, place not given*
   GAFNEY, John, from Ireland, laborer
   Major Wright's Corps
   Pass to Virginia
   *This deserter probably fought at Savannah, where Major Wright's troops were engaged.

060 1782 April --?, Quarterhouse
   WHITE, Joseph?, from North Carolina, farmer
   South Carolina Loyalists
   Pass to North Carolina

061 1782 April 08, James Island
   Three officers and 27 privates deserted [not named]
   Refugee Corps
   Passes [not reported]

062 1782 April 26, James Island
   GANNON?, James, from Ireland, farmer
   22nd? British Regiment
   Pass to Pennsylvania

063 1782 April 26, James Island
   McDONALD, John, from Ireland, weaver
   22nd? British Regiment
   Pass to Pennsylvania

064 1782 April 29, Quarterhouse
   WHITE, Daniel?, from Virginia, farmer
   South Carolina Loyalists
   Pass to North Carolina

065 1782 May 02, James Island
   HASE?/HARRIS?, James?, from Germany, farmer
   Regiment von Benning
   Pass to Pennsylvania
   Research Notes: (a) According to Hetrina, 1:4146, soldier HOSCH, Jakob [= James in English], born in 1753-1754, from Niederasphe, Hessen, deserted company 3, Regiment von Huyn, later von Benning, in May 1782. [Probable identification]
   (b) According to Ibid., 1:3795, soldier HESSE, Georg, born 1756-1757, from Gemuenden, Hessen, deserted company 4 of Regiment von Huyn, later von Benning, in January 1782; he then returned from Charleston to Long Island, NY, during the winter of 1782-1783. [Less likely identification]
   (c) According to Prussian census of 1871, Hessen-Nassau, Kreis Marburg, Landgemeinde Niederasphe. Total population 731 (all Protestant).
   (d) Geographic coordinates: 50-56N 8-40E, Hessen.
   (d) According to Preliminary Survey, the Family History Center, Salt Lake City, has Niederasphe Standesamt [civil] records, 1808-1811, and Oberasphe Buergermeisterei [mayoral] records for 1750-1847.

066 1782 May 02, James Island
   YOUNGMAN, H., from Germany, shopkeeper
   Regiment von Benning
   Pass to Pennsylvania
   Research Notes: (a) According to Hetrina, 1:4384, soldier JUNGERMANN, Henrich, born 1759-1760, from Neukirchen, Hessen, deserted from company 1 of Garrison Regiment von Huy, later von Benning, deserted in May 1782.
   (b) There are 27 villages of this name in West Germany, four in Hessen.
   (c) According to Preliminary Survey, the Family History Center, Salt Lake City, has Neukirchen/Ziegenhain Standesamt [civil registry] and Justizamt [court] records, 1768-1875.

067 1782 May 02, James Island
   KANAKA, Rud., from Germany, gardener
   Regiment von Ditfurth
   Pass to Pennsylvania
   Research Notes: (a) According to Hetrina, 4:1307, soldier KOENIG, Rudolf, born 1760-1761, from Witzenhausen, Hessen, deserted from the third company of the Feldjaeger Corps in August 1783. [Jaeger Corps members were frequently assigned to other troop units as sharpshooters, etc., and it may be that report of his defection from Regiment von Ditfurth did not reach his original unit until the following year. However, this identification is uncertain.]
   (b) According to the Prussian census of 1871, Hessen-Nassau, Regierungsbezirk Kassel, Kreis Witzenhausen, Stadtgemeinde Witzenhausen. Total population 3255 (2961 Protestants, 72 Catholics, 201 Jews).
   (c) There is also a Landgemeinde Witzenhausen-Bischhausen in the same Kreis. Its total population was 221 (all Protestant)
   (d) Geographic coordinates: 51-20N 9-52E Witzenhausen/Hessen; 51-21N 9-51E Witzenhausen-Bischhausen/Hessen.
   (e) According to Preliminary Survey, the Family History Center, Salt Lake City, has Witzenhausen

Amtsgericht [court] and Standesamt [civil registry] records for 1761-1874.

068 1782 May 02, James Island
PINKS, W[illia]m?, from Germany, weaver
Regiment von Benning
Pass to Pennsylvania
Research Notes: (a) According to <u>Hetrina</u>, 1:5738, soldier PFINGST, Wilhelm, born 1753-1754, from Viermuenden, Hessen, deserted from company 3 of Garrison Regiment von Huyn, later von Benning, in May 1782.
(b) According to the Prussian census of 1871, Hessen-Nassau, Regierungsbezirk Kassel, Kreis Frankenberg, Landgemeinde Viermuenden. Total population 472 (all Protestant).
(c) Geographic coordinates: 51-06N 8-49E Hessen.
(d) According to <u>Preliminary Survey</u>, the Family History Center, Salt Lake City, has Viermuenden Justizamt [court] records, 1734-1813.

069 1782 May 02, James Island
DEIKES, S., from Germany, carpenter
Regiment von Benning
Pass to Pennsylvania
Research Notes: (a) According to <u>Hetrina</u>, 1:2127, soldier DITTSCHAR, Stephan, born 1753-1754, from Itzenhain, Hessen, deserted from company 1 of Garrison Regiment von Huyn, latter von Benning, in May 1782. [Identification uncertain]
(b) According to the Prussian census of 1871, Hessen-Nassau, Kreis Ziegenhain, Landgemeinde Itzenhain. Total population 104 (all Protestants).
(c) Geographic coordinates 50-55N 9-04E.
(d) According to <u>Preliminary Survey</u>, the Family History Center, Salt Lake City, has Itzenhain Amtsgericht [court] records, 1833-1842.

070 1782 May 04, James Island
CRAWFORD, Arthur, from Ireland, bleacher
33rd British Regiment
Pass to Pennsylvania

071 1782 May 04, James Island
BROWN, Sand., from Ireland, weaver
33rd British Regiment
Pass ot Pennsylvania

072 1782 May 08, James Island
McKENNA?, John, from Scotland, tailor
Third? Regiment Guards
Pass to Philadelphia

073 1782 May 08, James Island
GREGORY, John, from England, sailor
<u>Viper</u> Galley
Pass to Philadelphia

074 1782 May 08, James Island
GRIFFY? William, from England, sailor
<u>Viper</u> Galley
Pass to Philadelphia

075 1782 May 10, James Island
GOODWIN, Thomas, from England, sailor
New York Volunteers
Pass to Philadelphia

076 1782 May 10, Stone [Stono?] River
JONES, J., from England, sailor
<u>Scorpion</u> Galley
Pass to Philadelphia

077 1782 May 09, James Island
WELKINSON, R., from England, sailmaker
New York Volunteers
Pass to Pennsylvania

078 1782 May 09, James Island
SOUTHERLAND, William, from Scotland, laborer
--? British Regiment
Pass to Pennsylvania

079 1782 May 09, James Island
McMULLEN, A., from Scotland, laborer
--? British Regiment
Pass to North Carolina

080 1782 May 21, James Island
STAR, Giles, from New England, sailor
<u>Adder</u> Galley
Pass to Georgetown

081 1782 May 20, Savannah
MITCHELL, J.?, from France, laborer
Col. Brown's [unit]
Pass to Virginia

082 1782 May 20, Augustine
PARKER, E., from North Carolina, cooper
60th British Regiment
Pass to North Carolina

083 1782 May 10, Savannah
LINCOLN, John, from Germany, sailor
Col. Fanning's? [unit]
Pass to Pennsylvania

084 1782 February 20, Augustine
PO---?, Francis, from Minorca, sailor
[No troop unit given]
Pass to Pennsylvania

085 1782 February 20, Augustine
SKEPELER, A., from Minorca, sailor
[Unit or ship not given]
Pass to Pennsylvania

086 1782 May 19, Savannah
CLEMENS, Henry, from Germany, laborer
Regiment von Knoblauch
Pass to Pennsylvania
Research Notes: (a) According to <u>Hetrina</u>,

3:2628, soldier CLEMENZ, Henrich, born 1749-1750, from Luxemburg, deserted from company 4, Garrison Regiment von Wissenbach, later von Knoblauch, in May 1782.

087 1782 May 24, Savannah
CROSS, John, from England, sailor
Fire Fly [Galley?]
Pass to Pennsylvania

088 1782 June 07, Quarterhouse
ELLMORE, William, from North Carolina, carpenter
Major Frazer's [Corps]
Pass to North Carolina

089 1782 June 07, Quarterhouse
FAIRES, John, from North Carolina, planter
Major Frazer's [Corps]
Pass to North Carolina

090 1782 June 07, Quarterhouse
COHOON, William, from North Carolina, planter
Major Frazer's [Corps]
Pass to North Carolina

091 1782 June 05, James Island
SCOTT, William, from Scotland, baker
Fifth? Regiment Guards
Pass to Philadelphia
Research Note: Deserters from the Fifth British Regiment have been reported in Clifford Neal Smith, British and German Deserters, Dischargees, and Prisoners of War Who May Have Remained in Canada and the United States, 1774-1783. British-American Genealogical Research Monograph Number 9, Part 1 (McNeal, AZ: Westland Publications, 1988). William Scott's name does not appear therein.

092 1782 June 05, James Island
SODEN?/LODEN?, William, from England, blacksmith
Fifth? Regiment Guards
Pass to Philadelphia
See Research Note for Number 091 above.

093 1782 June 05, James Island
THORNE, John, from England, shoemaker
Fifth? Regiment Guards
Pass to Philadelphia
See Research Note for Number 091 above.

094 1782 June 14, Quarterhouse
ATKINS, Thomas, from Virginia, carpenter
Major Frazer's Corps
Pass to Congaree

095 1782 June 14, James Island
BRADLEY, Esa, from Connecticut, farmer
Prince of Wales Regiment
Pass to Connecticut

096 1782 June 14, James Island
SCOFIELD, David, from [New?] Jersey, laborer
Prince of Wales Regiment
Pass to [New?] Jersey

097 1782 June 18, Quarterhouse
LASLIE, Peter, from South Carolina, farmer
Major Frazer's Corps
Pass to Broad River

098 1782 June 19, Quarterhouse
MULLEN?, John, Sergeant, from Ireland, sadler
Lord Rawdon's [Corps]
Pass to Philadelphia

099 1782 June 19, Quarterhouse
PORTER, Thomas, from Ireland, laborer
Lord Rawdon's [Corps]
Pass to Philadelphia

100 1782 June 19, Quarterhouse
McDONNOUCH, James, from Ireland, weaver
Lord Rawdon's [Corps]
Pass to Philadelphia

101 1782 June 19, Savannah
VISCHELL, Caspar, from Germany, weaver
Regiment von Knoblauch
Pass to Philadelphia
Research Notes: (a) According to Hetrina, 3:15950, soldier WETZEL/WITZEL, Kaspar, born 1754-55, from Breitenbach, Hessen, deserted from company 1, Garrison Regiment von Wissenbach, later von Knoblauch, in June 1782.
(b) There are 20 villages of this name in West Germany, 8 of them in Hessen.

102 1782 June 19, Savannah
CLEPROD, John, from Germany, wagoner
Regiment von Knoblauch
Pass to Philadelphia
Research Notes: According to Hetrina, 3:2485, soldier KLAPROT, Friedrich, born 1752-1753, from Osterode, a member of company 3, Regiment von Rall, was separated in Europe in October 1783. [This does not appear to be the same individual as the above, but Friedrich Klaprot is the only soldier listed of this surname and is mentioned here simply as a possible sibling.]

103 1782 June 25, Quarterhouse
McALLISTER?, Millington? Edward, from Ireland, laborer
Lord Rawdon's [Corps]
Pass to Pennsylvania

104 1782 June 20, Savannah
HART?/HERT?, Frederick, from Germany, blacksmith
Col. Campbell's Dragoons
Pass to Pennsylvania

105 1782 June 19, Savannah
PARIS, Joseph?, from New Spain, tailor
Col. Campbell's Dragoons
Pass to Pennsylvania
Research Comment: This surname might be PEREZ. It should be remembered that the Waldeck troops were in Louisiana during the Revolutionary War, when the region was part of New Spain. However, the surname does not appear in Hetrina, volume 5, which lists the Waldeck troops.

106 1782 June 30, James Island
SMITH, Anthony, from North Carolina, laborer
Refugee Corps
Pass to Broad River

107 1782 July 05, James Island
GORDON, James, from Scotland, barber
71st British Regiment
Pass to North Carolina

108 1782 July 05, James Island
TEED, David, Sergeant, from New York, tailor
New York Volunteers
Pass to New York state

109 1782 July 05, James Island
ELLISON, Charles, from England, laborer
New York Volunteers
Pass to Pennsylvania

110 1782 July 05, James Island
MARSHALL, Samuel?/James?, from England, barber
New York Volunteers
Pass to North Carolina

111 1782 July 05, James Island
ELLSWORTH, Samuel, American, carpenter
Prince of Wales Regiment
Pass to New York state

112 1782 July 05, James Island
ELLIOTT, David, from Ireland, laborer
Prince of Wales Regiment
Pass to New York state

113 1782 July 11, James Island
ROBINSON, James, prisoner, from Scotland, carpenter
82nd British Regiment
Pass to Philadelphia

114 1782 July 11, James Island
FULLERTON, James, prisoner, from Scotland, silk weaver
82nd British Regiment
Pass to Philadelphia

115 1782 July 12, Charleston
KENNEDY, William, American, farmer
Rattle Snake ship
Pass to Philadelphia

116 1782 July 11, Savannah
SHANNON, Patrick, from Ireland, house carpenter
[illegible, ship?]
Pass to Philadelphia

117 1782 July 11, Savannah
PITS, Samuel, from England, sailor
[illegible, ship?]
Pass to Philadelphia

118 1782 July 11, Savannah
DAWSONS, John, from England, sailor
[illegible, ship?]
Pass to Philadelphia

119 1782 July 15, Quarterhouse
TYLER, Owen, prisoner, from North Carolina, farmer
Col. Hamilton's [Corps]
Pass to North Carolina

120 1782 July 15, Quarterhouse
RYAL, Willis, from North Carolina, farmer
Captain Gilles' Regiment
Pass to North Carolina

121 1782 July 16, Quarterhouse
HOSERMAN?/KOSERMAN?, Bal[thasar], from Germany, laborer
Regiment von Angelelli
Pass to Virginia
Research Notes: (a) According to Hetrina, 3:2110, soldier CASSELMANN, Balthasar, born 1755-1756, from Westuffeln, Hessen, deserted from company 3, Regiment von Rall, latter von Angelelli, in July 1782; he had been a prisoner of war before February 1777.
(b) According to the Prussian census of 1871, Hessen-Nassau, Regierungsbezirk Kassel, Kreis Hofgeismar, Landgemeinde Westuffeln. Total population 717 (all Protestant).
(c) Geographic coordinates: 51-26N 9-20E Hessen.

122 1782 July 11, Savannah
MURRAY?/MURRY?, George, from Ireland, sailor
Ajourande [ship?]
Pass to Georgetown
Research Note: This might refer to the Adeljunde Luise, a ship which transported the Garrison Regiment von Wissenbach, later von Knoblauch, from Europe to New York early in the war. See Hetrina 3:0018 Introduction.

123 1782 July 11, Savannah
McCARTY, Daniel, American, sailor
Ajourande? [ship?]*
Pass to Georgetown
*See note at entry 122 above.

124 1782 July 11, Savannah
WILLIAMS, James, from Wales, sailor
Ajourande? [ship?]*
Pass to Georgetown
*See note at entry 122 above.

125 1782 July 11, Savannah
JONES, John, from England, sailor
Ajourande, [ship]*
Pass to Georgetown
*See note at entry 122 above.

126 1782 July 11, Savannah
PITTS?/POTTS?, Mack? Mark?, from South Carolina, laborer
Major Frazer's [Corps]
[illegible]

127 1782 July --?, Savannah
ACTIAN?, Brian, from Germany, barber
King's Rangers
Pass to Pennsylvania

128 1782 July 00?, Savannah
LEIDOFF, Herman, from Germany, potter
Regiment von Knoblauch
Pass to Pennsylvania
Research Notes: (a) According to Hetrina, 3:8935, soldier LEYDORF, Henrich, born 1749-1750, from Rotenberg, Hessen, deserted from company 5, Garrison Regiment von Wissenbach, later von Knoblauch, in July 1782.
(b) There are three villages of this name (Rotenberg) in West Germany, none in Hessen. However, Rotenburg in Niedersachsen is occasionally shown as Rotenberg.
(c) According to the Prussian census of 1871 Hessen-Nassau, Kreis Rotenburg, Stadtgemeinde Rotenburg an der Fulda. Total population 3275 (2787 Protestants, 162 Catholics, 323 Jews).
(d) According to Ibid., Provinz Hannover, Regierungsbezirk Stade, Kreis Rotenburg an der Wuemme, Amt Rotenburg. Total population 1770 (almost all Protestants).
(e) According to Preliminary Survey, the Family History Center, Salt Lake City, has Rothenberg/Hessen Evangelical church records, 1810-1975. They also have Rotenburg/Hessen Standesamt [civil registry], Amtsgericht [local court], and Evangelical church records, 1729-1964.

129 1782 July --?, Savannah
RINGLEBEN?, Martin, from Germany, shoemaker
Regiment von Knoblauch
Pass to Pennsylvania
Research Notes: (a) According to Hetrina, 3:11841, soldier RINGLEB, Martin, born 1759-1761, from Oberdorla, deserted from company 3, Garrison Regiment von Wissenbach, later von Knoblauch, in July 1782.
(b) Geographic coordinates: Oberdorla 51-10N 10-25E in Erfurt Regierungsbezirk of East Germany.

130 1782 July 13, Tybee
SAINTT, William, from England, sailor
Ajourande? [ship?]*
Pass to Philadelphia
*See note at entry 122 above.

131 1782 July 13, Tybee
YEO, James, from England, sailor
Ajourande? [ship]*
Pass to Philadelphia
*See note at entry 122 above.

132 1782 July 13
CO---? Tw---?, from Rostock?, sailor
Portsmouth transport [ship]
Pass to Philadelphia

133 1782 July 12, Savannah
ROCK, Henry, from Germany, tailor
[illegible]
Pass to Pennsylvania?

134 1782 July 29, --
CARSKADON?, James, from Ireland, farmer
[illegible]
Pass to New York state

135 1782 July 29, James Island
CARLOH?/SARLOH?, Thomas, from Pennsylvania, farmer
[illegible]
Pass to Pennsylvania

136 1782 July 26, Viper Galley
DOWNING, Edward, from England, chain turner
First Regiment Guards
Pass to Pennsylvania

137 1782 July 26, Viper Galley
HEIDER, Christian, Dane*, sailor
Viper Galley
Pass to Pennsylvania
*Possibly from Oldenburg, Schleswig, or Holstein, Germany, which at the time was subject to the Danish dynasty.

138 1782 July 26, Viper Galley
DUNIGAN, Thomas, from Ireland, weaver
33rd British Regiment
Pass to Pennsylvania

139 1782 July 27, Quarterhouse
WABERTON, Thomas, from England, weaver
23rd British Regiment
Pass to Pennsylvania

140 1782 July 27, Quarterhouse
PORTER, William, from England, baker
23rd British Regiment
Pass to Pennsylvania

141 1782 July 27, Quarterhouse
HEIDERMAN, Valentine, from Germany, farmer
Regiment de Benning
Pass to Pennsylvania
[continued]

Research Notes: (a) According to Hetrina, 1:3600, soldier HEINEMANN, Valentin, born 1759-1760, from Treysa, Hessen, deserted company 3, Garrison Regiment von Huyn, later von Benning, in July 1782. [Identification uncertain.]
(b) According to the Prussian census of 1871, Hessen-Nassau, Regierungsbezirk Kassel, Kreis Ziegenhain, Stadtgemeinde Treysa. Total population 2416 (2288 Protestants, 12 Catholics, 115 Jews).
(c) Geographic coordinates: Treysa 50-55N 9-12E. There is a village of Traisa at 49-50N 8-42E. Both villages are in Hessen.
(d) According to Preliminary Survey, the Family History Center, Salt Lake City, has Treysa Evangelical church and Justizamt [local court] records, 1567-1902.

142 1782 July 27, Quarterhouse
KESTLER, John*, from Germany, farmer
Regiment von Benning
Pass to Pennsylvania
*See also entry 145 below. (There were two men of this name who deserted.)
Research Notes: (a) According to Hetrina, 1:1188, soldier KESSLER, Johannes, born 1754-55, from Roeddenau, Hessen, deserted from company 3, Garrison Regiment von Huyn, later von Benning, in July 1782.
(b) According to the Prussian census of 1871, Hessen-Nassau, Regierungsbezirk Kassel, Kreis Frankenberg, Landgemeine Roeddenau. Total population 788 (768 Protestants, 11 Catholics, 8 Jews).
(c) Geographic coordinates: 51-03N 8-45E Hessen.
(d) According to Preliminary Survey, the Family History Center, Salt Lake City, has the Roeddenau Justizamt [local court] records, 1808-1873.

143 1782 July 14, Savannah
ZIMMER, Peter, from Germany, weaver
Regiment from Knoblauch
Pass to Pennsylvania
Research Notes: (a) According to Hetrina, 3:16570, soldier ZIMMER, Wilhelm, born 1759-60, from Sterkelshausen, Hessen, deserted from company 5, Garrison Regiment von Wissenbach, later von Knoblauch, in July 1782. [Identification uncertain]
(b) According to the Prussian census of 1871, Hessen-Nassua, Regierungsbezirk Kassel, Kreis Rotenberg an der Fulda, Landgemeinde Sterkelshausen. Total population 339 (all Protestant).
(c) Geographic coordinates: 51-00N 9-39E Hessen.
(d) According to Preliminary Survey, the Family History Center, Salt Lake City, has the Sterkelshausen Evangelical church records, 1658-1964.

144 1782 July 27, Quarterhouse
REEMAN?/KEEMAN?, Daniel, from Germany, blacksmith
Regiment von Angelelli
Pass to Pennsylvania
Research Notes: (a) According to Hetrina, 3:11768, soldier RIEMANN, Daniel, born 1755-1757, from Wollrode, Hessen, deserted from company 2, Regiment von Rall, later von Angelelli, in July 1782.
(b) According to the Prussian census of 1871, Hessen-Nassau, Regierungsbezirk Kassel, Kreis Melsungen, Landgemeinde Wollrode. Total population 319 (all Protestant).
(c) Geographic coordinates: 51-12N 9-30E, Hessen.
(d) According to Preliminary Survey, the Family History Center, Salt Lake City, has Wollrode Standesamt [civil registry] records, 1808-1812.

145 1782 July 27, Quarterhouse
KESTLER, John,* from Germany, gardener
Regiment von Benning
Pass to Pennsylvania
*See also entry 142 above. (There were two men of this name who deserted.)
Research Notes: (a) According to Hetrina, 1:1190, soldier KESSLER, Johannes, born 1754-1755, frm Rengershausen, Hessen, deserted from company 3, Garrison Regiment von Huyn, later von Benning, in July 1782.
(b) There are four villages of this name in West Germany, two of them in Hessen.
(c) According to the Prussian census of 1871:
 (i) Hessen-Nassau, Regierungsbezirk Kassel, Landkreis Kassel, Landgemeinde Rengershausen. Total population 380 (all Protestant).
 (ii) Hessen-Nassau, Regierungsbezirk Kassel, Kreis Frankenberg, Landgemeinde Rengershausen. Total population 303 (all Protestant).
(d) According to the Preliminary Survey, the Family History Center, Salt Lake City, has Rangershausen* Justizamt [local court] records for 1802-1846.
*So spelled.

146 1782 July 25, Quarterhouse
BAKER, John, from Germany, farmer
Regiment von Ditfurth
Pass to Pennsylvania
Research Notes: (a) According to Hetrina, 2:0633, soldier BECKER, Johannes, born 1750-1751, from Marbach, Hessen, deserted from company 1, Regiment von Ditfurth, in July 1782.
(b) There are seventeen villages of this name in West Germany, two in Hessen.
(c) According to the Prussian census of 1871, (i) Hessen-Kassel, Regierungsbezirk Kassel, Kreis Marburg, Landgemeinde Marbach. Total population 262 (all Protestant).
(ii) Hessen-Kassel, Kreis Fulda, Landgemeinde Marbach. Total population 578 (565 Catholic, 13 Protestant).
(d) Geographic coordinates: 50-37N 9-43E and 50-49N 8-45E, both in Hessen.

147 1782 July 28, Quarterhouse
MOSER, Lawrence, from Germany, butcher
Regiment von Angelelli
Pass to Pennsylvania
Research Notes: (a) According to Hetrina, 3:10124, soldier MOSER, Lorenz, born 1754-1756, from Grosskorbach/Pfalz, deserted from company 2 of Regiment von Rall in July 1782. (He had been wounded before September 1779 and was under arrest in his regiment from before November 1781

to May 1782, when released. He then defected in July 1782.)
(b) Grosskarbach has not been found. However, there is a Grosskarlbach/Pfalz.
(c) According to Prussian census of 1871, Provinz Rheinland, Regierungsbezirk Koblenz, Kreis Sankt Goar, Buergermeisterei Halsenbach, Landgemeinde Karbach. Total population 423 (all Catholics). [This is only a tentative identification of this village. The church for this village was in Halsenbach.]
(d) According to Preliminary Survey, the Family History Center, Salt Lake City, has Grosskarlbach/Pfalz Evangelical and Catholic church records, 1707-1888.
(e) According to Ibid., the Halsenbach Catholic church records from 1669-1909 are also available.

148 1782 July 28, Quarterhouse
HANDKAMMER?, Philip, from Germany, farmer
Regiment von Angelelli
Pass to Pennsylvania
Research Notes: (a) According to Hetrina, 3:6804, soldier HANDKAMMER, Philipp, born 1756-1757, from Wehrdorf or Werdorf, deserted from company 2, Regiment von Rall, later von Angelelli, in July 1782.
(b) There are no villages of Wehrdorf named in modern sources. There is a village of Werdorf, geographic coordinates: 50-36N 8-24E in Hessen, but it is not listed in the Prussian census of 1871.

149 1782 July 28, James Island
MURRAY, Hugh, from Ireland, weaver
New York Volunteers
Pass to Pennsylvania

150 1782 July 29, Quarterhouse
MITZNER, Jost, from Germany, blacksmith
Regiment von Benning
Pass to Pennsylvania
Research Notes: (a) According to Hetrina, 1:5360, soldier MUETZE, Johannes, born 1754-1755, from Birkenbringhausen, Hessen, deserted from company 3, Garrison Regiment von Huyn, later von Benning, in July 1782. (A possible sibling reenlisted in Regiment von Rall in 1783, after the Revolution.)
(b) According to the Prussian census of 1871 there are two rural villages named Bringhausen an der Birken and Bringhausen an der Edder. Both were in Hessen-Nassau, Regierungsbezirk Kassel, Kreis Frankenberg. Residents of both villages were Protestants.
(c) Geographic coordinates: 51-01N 8-44E Hessen.

151 1782 July 30, Quarterhouse
McDOUGAL, Randle, from South? Carolina, farmer
Major? Martin's Corps
Pass to South? Carolina

152 1782 July 30, Quarterhouse
WITT?, Wohrin?/Wilh.?, from Germany, butcher
Regiment von Angelelli
Pass to Philadelphia
Research Comment: According to Hetrina, 3:16328, soldier WITT, Joachim, born 1738-1741, from Stralsund, deserted from company 2, Regiment von Rall, later Angelelli, in July 1782. [Identification uncertain].
(b) Geographic coordinates: Stralsund 54-18N 13-06E Regierungsbezirk Rostock in East Germany.
(c) According to Preliminary Survey, the Family History Center, Salt Lake City, has Stralsund military church books, 1818-1860, and Kriegsratgerichte [military court records], 1705-1890.

153 1782 July 30, Quarterhouse
DOER, Gollip?, from Germany, tailor
Regiment von Angelelli
Pass to Philadelphia
Research Notes: According to Hetrina, 3:14798, soldier THORER, Gottlieb, born 1754-1760, from Gera, deserted from company 2, Regiment von Rall, later von Angelelli, in July 1782.
(b) Geographic coordinates: 50-52N 12-05E Regierungsbezirk Gera, East Germany.

154 1782 August 01, Quarterhouse
MILLER, Otto, from Germany, shoemaker
Regiment von Angelelli
Pass to Philadelphia
Research Note: No soldier of this given name could be found in Hetrina; however, there were others of this surname who defected.

155 1782 August --?, St. John's River
CARSON, Robert, from Ireland, sailor
Lovely Cass [ship?]
Pass to Georgetown

156 1782 August 06, Quarterhouse
WHITLOCK, James, from New Jersey, tailor
King's Rangers
Pass to Philadelphia

157 1782 August 06, Quarterhouse
FANNING, Peter, from Ireland, no occupation
King's Rangers
Pass to Philadelphia

158 1782 August 07, James Island
FLAGLER, William, from New York state?, farmer
New York Volunteers
Pass to New York state

159 1782 August 07, James Island
LEATE?/TEATE?, Benjamin, Sergeant, from New York state?, farmer
New York Volunteer Corps
Pass to New York state

160 1782 August 07, James Island
BATES, Joseph, Sergeant, from New York state?, farmer
New York Volunteer Corps
Pass to New York state

161 1782 August 07, James Island
WAITE, Thomas, Sergeant, from Massachusetts, farmer
New York Volunteer Corps
Pass to New York state

162 1782 August 08, James Island
   MOTT?, Richard, private?, from New York, farmer
   New York Volunteer Corps
   Pass to New York state

163 1782 August 08, James Island
   HAYNES?, James, private?, from New York, weaver
   New York Volunteer Corps
   Pass to New York state

164 1782 August 08, James Island
   CONWAY, Jeremiah, Dragoon, from South Carolina, farmer
   Major Fraser's? Corps
   Pass to Peedee? River, South Carolina

165 1782 August 08, James Island
   CONWAY, William, from South Carolina, farmer
   Major Fraser's? Corps
   Pass to Peedee? River, South Carolina

166 1782 August 04, Savannah
   BARUCH?/BAUCH?, Nicholas, private, from Germany, mason
   Regiment von Knoblauch
   Pass to Philadelphia
   Research Notes: (a) According to Hetrina, 3:0529, soldier BAUCKER, Nikolaus, born 1754-1755, from Gamlen/Jammeln or Gommla/Jammeln, deserted from company 4, Garrison Regiment von Wissenbach, later von Knoblauch, in June 1782.
   (b) No village named Gamlen has been found; however, there is a village named Jameln at coordinates 53-03N 11-05E in Niedersachsen, West Germany; there is a village named Gommlo at 51-44 12-30E in Halle Regierungsbezirk of East Germany.

167 1782 August 09, Charleston
   CALLY, William, from South Carolina, farmer
   Major Fraser's Corps
   Pass to Ninety-Six

168 1782 August 09, James Island
   CALDWELL, William, from Virginia, sadler
   Frigate Carolina, joined the Artificers
   Pass destination not given

169 1782 August 09, Charleston
   WORKSMAN, Daniel, from Ireland, farmer
   Major Fraser's Corps
   Pass to Ninety-Six District

170 1782 Augus 10, James Island
   GLENN, Robert, from Virginia, millwright
   Major Fraser's Corps
   Pass to Ninety-Six District

171 1782 August 09, Charleston
   McDONALD, Hugh, from Scotland, farmer
   George Martin's [Corps]
   Pass destination not given

172 1782 August 09, Charleston
   McDONALD, Paul, from Scotland, farmer
   George Martin's [Corps]
   Pass to North Carolina

173 1782 August 09, Charleston
   McDONALD, Donald, from Scotland, farmer
   George Martin's [Corps]
   Pass to North Carolina

174 1782 August 11, Charleston
   DONALD?/McDONALD?, John, Sergeant, from Virginia, farmer
   Major Fraser's [Corps]
   Pass to Broad River, South? Carolina

175 1782 August 11, Charleston
   JACKSON, James, from South Carolina, farmer
   Major Fraser's [Corps]
   Pass to Broad River, South? Carolina

176 1782 August --?, place not given
   VERNON?/VERNER?, James, from South Carolina, farmer
   Major Fraser's [Corps]
   Pass to Broad River

177 1782 August --?, place not given
   HOLMES, James?/Talman?, from North Carolina, farmer
   Major Fraser's [Corps]
   Pass to North Carolina

178 1782 August --?, place not given
   DAILY, James, from South Carolina, farmer
   Major Fraser's [Corps]
   Pass to Broad River

179 1782 August 14, place not given
   DIXON, William, from South Carolina, farmer
   Col. Bevan's? [corps]
   Pass to Broad River

180 1782 August 17, Charleston
   LEIBRA?/SEIBRI?, A. F., from France, shoemaker
   Col. Bevan's? [Corps]
   Pass to Augusta

181 1782 August 17, Charleston
   CARLESTON?, Thomas, from Augusta, farmer
   Col. Bevan's? [Corps]
   Pass to Augusta

182 1782 August 17, Charleston
   ULM, Joseph?, from Germany, mason
   Regiment von Ditfurth
   Pass destination not given
   Research Notes: According to Hetrina, 2:11044, soldier ULM, Josef, no birth year given, from Metz [France], deserted from company 3, Regiment von Ditfurth, in August 1782.

183 1782 August 17, James Island
ROBERTSON, Robert, from Scotland, farmer
71st British Regiment
Pass to Wilmington, Delaware?

184 1782 August 17, James Island
McCREA, Kenneth, from Scotland, farmer
7th?/71st? British Regiment
Pass to Virginia

185 1782 August 19, James Island
ESELMAN, James, from Scotland, weaver
82nd British Regiment
Pass to Philadelphia

186 1782 August 20, Charleston
WHITMAN, Richard?, corporal, from Virginia, farmer
King's Rangers
Pass to Virginia

187 1782 August 20, Charleston
THOMPSON, Robert, from Virginia, joiner
King's Rangers
Pass to Virginia

188 1782 August 20, Charleston
HAWKINS, Samuel, from Virginia, farmer
King's Rangers
Pass to Augusta

189 1782 August 20, Charleston
CLARK, William, from Virginia, farmer
King's Rangers
Pass to Augusta

190 1782 August 27, Charleston
WILSON, William, from South Carolina, farmer
Lt. Col. Hamilton's?/Merritt's? [Corps]
Pass to Camden

191 1782 August 27, Charleston
STEVENSON, James?/John?, from Maryland, farmer
Lt. Col. Hamilton's?/Merritt's? [Corps]
Pass to Maryland

192 1782 August 29, Charleston
DEFERT?, William, from Virginia, farmer
Lt. Col. Hamilton's [Corps]
Pass to Orangeburgh?

193 1782 August 29, Charleston
DEFOOTE?, Daniel?/Samuel?, from South Carolina, farmer
Lt. Col. Hamilton's [Corps]
Pass to Orangeburgh?

194 1782 August 29, Charleston
GUTMUTH?, Daniel?, from Germany, farmer
Lt. Col. Hamilton's [Corps]
Pass to Orangeburgh?

195 1782 August 30, James Island
MAZICK?, Elisha?, from Maryland, farmer
Prince of Wales Regiment
Pass to Maryland

196 1782 August 30, James Island
GASSAT, Joseph, from North Carolina, farmer
Prince of Wales Regiment
Pass to North Carolina

197 1782 August 25, Quarterhouse?
NIXON, James, from Ireland, farmer
84th British Regiment
Pass to Pennsylvania

198 1782 August 31, Charleston
STEIMBY?, Abraham, from New York, cooper
New York Volunteers
Pass to New York

199 1782 August 31, Charleston
MOSES, Stephen, Sergeant, from New York, farmer
New York Volunteers
Pass to New York

200 1782 August 31, James Island
STOREF?/STOUF?, Henry, from Germany, sutler
Regiment von Ditfurth
Pass to North Carolina
Research Notes: (a) According to Hetrina, 2:10435, soldier STAUB, Henrich, born 1751-1752, from Buergeln, Hessen, deserted from company 2, Regiment von Ditfurth, in September 1782. (Note also that, in Ibid., 2:10436, soldier STAUB, Johannes, enlisted in the same company, Regiment von Ditfurth, in 1783 (month not given). It may be that Henry and Johannes are the same person, since most German men of the time period had Johannes as one of their given names. Thus, if both entries refer to the same soldier, it would indicate that Henry may not have been a deserter but a prisoner of war returning to his regiment.)
(b) According to the Prussian census of 1871, Hessen-Nassau, Regierungsbezirk Kassel, Kreis Marburg, Landgemeinde Buergel [so spelled]. Total population 438 (almost all Protestant).
(c) According to Preliminary Survey, the Family History Center, Salt Lake City, has Buergeln police records, 1808-1867.

201 1782 September --?, Charleston
LONG, William, from Virginia, farmer
Col. Brown's [Corps]
Pass destination not given

202 1782 September --?, Charleston
STERNS?, John, from Maryland, shoemaker
Col. Brown's [Corps]
Pass to Broad River

203 1782 September 03, Charleston
TAYLOR, Richard, from England, plasterer
63rd British Regiment
Pass to Philadelphia

204 1782 September 02, Charleston
SCOFIELD, Richard, from England, miller
23rd British Regiment
Pass to Philadelphia

205 1782 September 02, Charleston
SIMMONS?, Richard, from England, brickmaker
23rd British Regiment
Pass to Philadelphia

206 1782 September 03, Charleston
WRIGHT, Mitchel?, from Germany, weaver
Regiment von Ditfurth
Pass to Pennsylvania
Research Notes: (a) According to Hetrina, 2:8263, soldier REITH, Michael, born 1754-1756, from Marburg, Hessen, deserted company 4, Regiment von Ditfurth, in September 1782.
(b) According to the Prussian census of 1871, Hessen-Nassau, Regierungsbezirk Kassel, Kreis Marburg, Stadtgemeinde Marburg. Total population 8950 (8062 Protestants, 695 Catholics, 166 Jews).
(c) Geographic coordinates: 50-49N 8-46E, Hessen.
(d) According to the Preliminary Survey the Family History Center, Salt Lake City, has massive records from Marburg: court records, 1698-1890; church records and Sippenbuch [lineage records], 1500-1850; Standesamt and Justizamt, 1808-1883.

207 1782 September 03, Charleston
LISHER?/FISCHER/SISCHER?, Gas--r, from Germany, farmer
Regiment von Ditfurth
Pass to Pennsylvania
Research Notes: (a) According to Hetrina, 2:6176, soldier LEISGE, Kaspar, born 1750-1751, from Todenhausen, Hessen, deserted from company 4, Regiment von Ditfurth, in September 1782.
(b) There are two villages of this name, both in Hessen. According to the Prussian census of 1871:
(i) Hessen-Nassau, Regierungsbezirk Kassel, Kreis Marburg, Landgemeinde Todenhausen (Deutsch). Total population 254 (all Protestant).
(ii) Hessen-Nassau, Regierungsbezirk Kassel, Kreis Ziegenhain, Landgemeinde Todenhausen. Total population 292 (all Protestant).
(c) Geographic coordinates: 50-55N 8-42E and 50-58N 9-18E, both Hessen.

208 1782 September 3, Charleston
CHARLES, Henry, from Germany, barber
Regiment von Angelelli
Pass to Pennsylvania
Research Notes: (a) According to Hetrina, 3:2096, soldier CARLE, Henrich, born 1757-1758, from Doernberg, Hessen, deserted company 4, Regiment von Rall, later Angelelli, in September 1782.
(b) There are several villages of this name in West Germany, two in Hessen; also Doernberg'scher Hof.
(c) According to the Prussian census of 1871,
(i) Hessen-Nassau, Regierungsbezirk Kassel, Kreis Wolfhagen, Landgemeinde Doernberg. Total population 867 (all Protestant).
(ii) Hessen-Nassau, Regierungsbezirk Wiesbaden, Unterlahnkreis, Amt Diez, Landgemeinde Doernberg. Total population 505 (420 Protestants, 79 Catholics).
(iii) Hessen-Nassau, Regierungsbezirk Kassel, Kreis Ziegenhain, Doernberg'scher Ritterhof [noble estate] near the village of Hausen.

209 1782 September 04, Charleston
STUART, Randle, from Scotland, farmer
George Martin's [Corps]
Pass to North Carolina

210 1782 September 04, Charleston
McDONALD, H., drummer, from Scotland, farmer
George Martin's [Corps]
Pass to North Carolina

211 1782 September 04, Charleston
McCOY, William, from Scotland, farmer
George Martin's [Corps]
Pass to North Carolina

212 1782 September 04, James Island
VAUGHAN, Hugh, from Ireland, hairdresser
Prince of Wales [Regiment]
Pass to Philadelphia

213 1782 September 05, Charleston
MYERS, Harmon, drummer, from Germany, shoemaker
Regiment von Angelelli
Pass to Pennsylvania
Research Notes: (a) According to Hetrina, 3:9862, soldier MEYER, Hermann, drummer, born 1750-1760, from Homberg, deserted from company 4, Regiment von Rall, later von Angelelli, in September 1782.
(b) There are ten villages named Homberg in West Germany, two in Hessen.
(c) According to the Prussian census of 1871:
(i) Hessen-Nassau, Regierungsbezirk Kassel, Kreis Homberg, Stadtgemeinde Homberg. Total population 3001 (2968 Protestant, 26 Catholics).
(ii) Hessen-Nassau, Regierungsbezirk Wiesbaden, Kreis Oberwesterwald, landgemeinde Homberg. Total population 176 (all Protestant).
(d) According to the Preliminary Survey, the Family History Center, Salt Lake City, has Homberg/Alsfeld church records, 1808-1875; Homberg/Kassel Justizamt [local court] records, 1816-1867; and Homberg/Fritslar Justizamt and Landgemeinde [communal] records, 1733-1880.

214 1782 September 05, Charleston
CRITZBURGH, Conrad, from Germany, farmer
Regiment von Angelelli
Pass to Pennsylvania
Research Notes: (a) According to Hetrina, 3:3457, soldier CREUTZBERG, Konrad, born 1761-1764, from Iba, Hessen, deserted company 1, Regiment von Rall, later von Angelelli, in September 1782.
(b) According to the Prussian census of 1871 Hessen-Nassau, Regierungsbezirk Kassel, Kreis Rotenberg, Landgemeinde Iba. Total population 830 (815 Protestants, 14 Jews).
(c) Geographic coordinates: 50-58N 9-52E Hessen.
(d) According to the Preliminary Survey, the Family History Center, Salt Lake City, has Iba Standesamt [civil registry] records, 1808-1875.

215 1782 September 05, James Island
WADSWORTH, William, from North Carolina, farmer
[Major] Fraser's Corps
Pass to North Carolina

216 1782 September 07, Charleston
MONRO, Richard, from Lancashire, Old England, millwright
Farley Transport [ship]
Pass to Pennsylvania

217 1782 September 09, Charleston
BEARD, Henry, from Virginia, farmer
Major Fraser's [Corps]
Pass to Virginia

218 1782 September 09, Charleston
JACKSON, John, from South Carolina, farmer
Major Fraser's [Corps]
Pass to Ninety-Six, South Carolina

219 1782 September 09, Charleston
CORNELL?/CONNELL?, Arthur, from Virginia, farmer
Major Fraser's [Corps]
Pass to Virginia

220 1782 September 03, St. Helena, Pt.? Royal
WOODWARD, David, from Connecticut, carpenter
Fanning's Regiment
Pass to New York

221 1782 September 11, James Island
JOHNSTONE, Peter, from Scotland, farmer
71st British Regiment
Pass to Pennsylvania

222 1782 September 10, Charleston
ARTIS, John, from Great Britain, farmer
Col. Hamilton's [Corps]
Pass to Virginia

223 1782 September 12, Charleston?
ALEXANDER, Robert, from Ireland, fuller
Lord Rawdon's [Corps]
Pass to North Carolina

224 1782 September 12, Charleston
AMICK, Adam, from South Carolina, farmer
[Major] Fraser's Corps
Pass to Broad and Salada rivers, South Carolina

225 1782 September 12, Charleston
SUTTES?, Martin, from South Carolina, farmer
[Major] Fraser's Corps
Pass to Broad and Salada rivers, South Carolina

226 1782 September 12, Charleston
SEITZLER, Adam, from Germany, farmer
[Major] Fraser's Corps
Pass to Broad and Salada rivers, South Carolina

227 1782 September 12, Charleston
GITSINGER, Benjamin, from South Carolina, farmer
[Major] Fraser's Corps
Pass to Broad and Salada rivers, South Carolina

228 1782 September 11, Charleston
NORRIS, William, from Virginia, farmer
[Colonel] Hamilton's Regiment
Pass to North Carolina

229 1782 September 11, Charleston
VEITCH, Elias, from Maryland, farmer
[Colonel] Hamilton's [Corps]
Pass to North Carolina

230 1782 September 11, Charleston
ROYER?/REZAR?/RYAN?, Charles, from North Carolina, farmer
[Colonel] Hamilton's [Corps]
Pass to North Carolina

231 1782 September 11, Charleston
ROYER?/REZAR?/RYAN?, William, from Virginia, farmer
[Colonel] Hamilton's [Corps]
Pass to --? [North Carolina?]

232 1782 September 05, Charleston
McMULLIN?, Thomas, from Ireland, tailor
[Major] Fraser's [Corps]
Pass to Ninety-Six District

233 1782 September 12, Charleston
BENNET?, Elisha?, from New England, farmer
Fanning's [Regiment]
Pass to [New] York state

234 1782 September 13, Wasag? cutz--?
MATHEWS, John, from Pennsylvania, sailor
Trimmer? Galley
Pass to Philadelphia

235 1782 September 12, Charleston
HOFMASTER, William, from Germany, farmer
Regiment von Ditfurth
Pass to Pennsylvania
Research Notes: (a) According to Hetrina, 2:5571, soldier HOFMEISTER, Wilhelm, born 1752-1753, from Somplar, Hessen, deserted from company 4, Regiment von Ditfurth, in September 1782.
(b) According to the Prussian census of 1871 Hessen-Nassau, Regierungsbezirk Kassel, Kreis Frankenberg, Landgemeinde Somplar. Total population 295 (all Protestant).
(c) Geographic coordinates: 51-06N 8-40E, Hessen.

236 1782 September 12, Charleston
SOLTER, Hammond, from Germany, farmer
Regiment von Ditfurth
Pass to Pennsylvania
Research Notes: (a) According to Hetrina, 2:10270, soldier SOLDAN/SULTHAN, Hermann, born

1755-1756, from Muenchhausen, Hessen, deserted from company 4, Regiment von Ditfurth, in September 1782.
(b) According to the Prussian census of 1871, there are two villages of Muenchhausen in Hessen:
  (i) Hessen-Nassau, Regierungsbezirk Kassel, Kreis Marburg, Landgemeinde Muenchhausen. Total population 946 (all Protestant).
  (ii) Hessen-Nassau, Regierungsbezirk Wiesbaden, Dillkreis, Landgemeinde Muenchhausen. Total population 302 (all Protestant).
(c) Geographic coordinates: 50-37N 8-12E and 50-57N 8-43E, both in Hessen
(d) According to the Preliminary Survey, the Family History Center, Salt Lake City, has Muenchhausen/Marburg Standesamt [civil registry] records, 1808-1813.

237 1782 September 12, Charleston
SPOTZ, Caspar, from Germany, farmer
Regiment von Ditfurth
Pass to Pennsylvania
Research Notes: (a) According to Hetrina, 2:9030, soldier SCHATZ, Kaspar, born 1758-1759, from Bromskirchen, deserted from company 4, Regiment von Ditfurth, in September 1782.
(b) According to the Prussian census of 1871, Hessen-Nassau, Regierungsbezirk Wiesbaden, Hinterlandkreis (Biedenkopf), Landgemeinde Bromskirchen. Total population 936 (913 Protestants, 21 Jews).
(c) Geographic coordinates: 51-05N 8-37E, Hessen.
(d) According to the Preliminary Survey, the Family History Center, Salt Lake City, has Bromskirchen Evangelical church records and Justizamt [local court] records, 1808-1874.

238 1782 September 13, Coles Island
FISHER, Charles, from England, cotton weaver
[Colonel] Hamilton's [Corps]
Pass to Philadelphia

239 1782 September 13, Coles Island
MORGAN, Michael, from England, ships carpenter
[Colonel] Hamilton's [Corps]
Pass to Philadelphia

240 1782 September 13, Coles Island
LANMAN?/SANMAN?, John, from Virginia, farmer
George Martin's [Corps]
Pass to Maryland

241 1782 September 13, Charleston
McELROY, Henry, from New York state, smith
King's Rangers
Pass to [New] York state

242 1782 September 05, Charleston
GOSLING, William J., from Guernsey, seaman
Vulture, Sloop of War
Pass to Maryland

243 1782 September 18, James Island
FOOT, John, Ireland, shoemaker
82nd British Regiment
Pass to Pennsylvania

244 1782 September 22, James Island
McLANE, John, from Scotland, farmer
71st British Regiment
Pass to Pennsylvania

245 1782 September 21, Charleston
LINKER, Henry, from Germany, farmer
Regiment von Ditfurth
Pass to Virginia
Research Notes: (a) According to Hetrina, 2:6304, soldier LINCKER, Henrich, born 1750-1751, from Erksdorf, Hessen, deserted company 3, Regiment von Ditfurth, in September 1782.
(b) This village is not listed in the Prussian census of 1871.
(c) Geographic coordinates: 50-51N 9-01E, Hessen.
(d) According to the Preliminary Survey, the Family History Center, Salt Lake Center, has Erksdorf Standesamt [civil registry] records, 1808-1874.

246 1782 July 09, Savannah
JACOB, Herman, Sergeant, from Germany, shoemaker
Regiment von Knoblauch
Pass to Virginia
Research Notes: (a) According to Hetrina, 3:8498, soldier JAKOB, Hermann, Sergeant, no birth year given, from Homberg, deserted from Garrison Regiment von Wissenbach, later von Knoblauch, in June 1782.
(b) For Homberg/Hessen, see Entry 213 above.

247 1782 September 18, Charleston
McLAUGHLIN, James, from England, barber
63rd British Regiment
Pass to Georgetown

248 1782 September 27, Charleston
GEORGE, David, from Virginia, farmer
Major Fraser's [Corps]
Pass to Ninety-Six District

249 1782 September 27, Charleston
CARMAN, Samuel, from Maryland, farmer
Major Fraser's [Corps]
Pass to North Carolina

250 1782 September 27, Charleston
BROWN, Thomas, from North Carolina, farmer
Major Fraser's [Corps]
Pass to North Carolina

251 1782 September 27, Charleston
HEATH, James, from North Carolina, farmer
Major Fraser's [Corps]
Pass to North Carolina

252 1782 September 27, Charleston
HEATH, Richard, from North Carolina, farmer
Major Fraser's [Corps]
Pass to North Carolina

253 1782 September 27, Charleston
   KENT, Levi, from Virginia, farmer
   Major Fraser's [Corps]
   Pass to North Carolina

254 1782 September 27, Charleston
   ALLANTHORPE?, Priestly, from South Carolina, farmer
   Major Fraser's [Corps]
   Pass to Broad River

255 1782 September 27, Charleston
   TREWIT?, Samuel, from North Carolina, cooper
   Major Fraser's [Corps]
   Pass to North Carolina

256 1782 September 28, Charleston
   McKENZIE, Andrew, Sergeant, from Ireland, weaver
   North Carolina Loyalists
   Pass to North Carolina

257 1782 September 28, Charleston
   McKAY, Richard?, Corporal, from Scotland, farmer
   North Carolina Loyalists
   Pass to North Carolina

258 1782 September 28, Johns Island
   JACKSON, Thomas, from Virginia?, farmer
   Major Fraser's [Corps]
   Pass to Virginia

259 1782 September 28, Johns Island
   WATKINS, John, from Virginia, farmer
   Major Fraser's [Corps]
   Pass to Virginia

260 1782 September 28, Johns Island
   WATKINS, William, from Virginia, farmer
   Major Fraser's [Corps]
   Pass to Virginia

261 1782 September 29, Charleston
   SIMS, Isaac, from Virginia, farmer
   North Carolina Loyalists
   Pass to Virginia

262 1782 September 20, Charleston
   WALTERS?/WALTON?, William, from Connecticut, tanner?/farmer?
   De Lancy's? [Corps]
   Pass to Connecticut

263 1782 September 29, Charleston
   WHEELER, Benjamin, from Connecticut, farmer
   De Lancy's? [Corps]
   Pass to Connecticut

264 1782 September 02, James Island
   CROMER, Michael, from Germany, farmer
   Major Fraser's [Corps]
   Pass to Broad River

265 1782 September 02, James Island
   LAND?, William, from North Carolina, farmer
   Major Fraser's [Corps]
   Pass to North Carolina

266 1782 October 03, James Island
   [illegible], John, Sergeant?, from Connecticut, farmer
   Prince of Wales Regiment
   Pass to North Carolina

267 1782 October 03, James Island
   CROFORD, [illegible], Sergeant?, from Connecticut, farmer
   Prince of Wales Regiment
   Pass to North Carolina

268 1782 October 03, James Island
   PATTERSON, Hugo?, from Connecticut, farmer
   Prince of Wales Regiment
   Pass to North Carolina

269 1782 October 04, Charleston
   McCULLOP?, David, from Scotland, farmer
   71st British Regiment
   Pass to Pennsylvania

270 1782 October 04, Charleston
   McLAUGHLIN, Patrick?/Peter?, from Scotland, farmer
   71st British Regiment
   Pass to Pennsylvania

271 1782 October 06, Johns Island
   JACKSON, Daniel, Sergeant, from Connecticut, farmer
   Prince of Wales Regiment
   Pass to Connecticut

272 1782 October 06, Johns Island
   HIGGS, Jesse, from Maryland, farmer
   New York Volunteers
   Pass to Maryland

273 1782 October 06, Johns Island
   SMETHERS, John, from New York, shoemaker
   Prince of Wales Regiment
   Pass to New York

274 1782 October 09, Savannah
   WALTER, Joseph, from Germany, weaver
   Regiment von Knoblauch
   Pass to Pennsylvania
   Research Notes: (a) According to Hetrina, 3:15524, soldier WALTER, Justus, born 1753-1754, from Burghofen, Hessen, deserted from company 3 of the Garrison Regiment von Wissenbach, later von Knoblauch, in July 1782.
   (b) According to the Prussian census of 1871, Hessen-Nassau, Regierungsbezirk Kassel, Kreis Eschwege, Landgemeinde Burghofen. Total population 219 (all Protestants).
   (c) Geographic coordinates: 51-07N 9-50E Hessen.

275 1782 October 09, Savannah
LAPS?, John Wollen?/William?, from Germany, weaver
Regiment von Knoblauch
Pass to Pennsylvania
Research Notes: (a) According to Hetrina, 3:16427, soldier WOLLENHAUPT, Johannes, born 1753-1754, from Pfieffe, Hessen, deserted from company 3, Garrison Regiment von Wissenhaupt, later von Knoblauch, in July 1782. [Identification uncertain]
(b) According to the Prussian census of 1871, Hessen-Nassau, Regierungsbezirk Kassel, Kreis Melsungen, Landgemeinde Pfieffe. Total population 486 (all Protestant).
(c) Geographic coordinates: 51-06N 9-44E Hessen.
(d) According to the Preliminary Survey, the Family History Center, Salt Lake City, has Pfieffe communal and Standesamt [civil registry] records, 1808-1886.

276 1782 October 07, Savannah
WINTERBOTTOM, John, from England, farmer
33rd British Regiment
Pass to Camden

277 1782 October 07, Charleston
KIMBALL?, John Yost, from Germany, farmer
Regiment von Benning
Pass to Camden
Research Notes: (a) According to Hetrina, 1:2984, soldier GIMBEL, Jost, born 1757-1758, from Gemuenden, Hessen, deserted from company 4, Garrison Regiment von Huyn, later von Benning, in October 1782.
(b) There are five villages of this name in West Germany, three in Hessen.
(c) According to the Prussian census of 1871:
  (i) Hessen-Nassau, Regierungsbezirk Kassel, Kreis Frankenberg, Stadtgemeinde Gemuenden. Total population 1330 (1259 Protestants, 70 Jews).
  (ii) Hessen-Nassau, Regierungsbezirk Wiesbaden, Kreis Oberwesterwald, Amt Rennerod, Landgemeinde Gemuenden. Total population 1014 (953 Protestants, 12 Catholics, 48 Jews).
  (iii) Hessen-Nassau, Regierungsbezirk Wiesbaden, Kreis Obertaunus, Amt Usingen, Landgemeinde Gemuenden. Total population 284 (all Protestant).
(d) Geographic coordinates: 50-22N 8-25E, Hessen.
(e) According to the Preliminary Survey, the Family History Center, Salt Lake City, has Gemuenden/Frankenberg Standesamt [civil registry] and Justizamt [local court] records, 1808-1884.

278 1782 October 07, Charleston
BRUNAMAN?, Abraham, from Germany, farmer
Regiment von Benning
Pass to Camden
Research Notes: (a) According to Hetrina, 1:764, soldier BORNMANN, Abraham, born 1755-1756, from Gemuenden, Hessen, deserted from company 4, Garrison Regiment von Huyn, later von Benning, in October 1782.
(b) For Gemuenden/Hessen, see Entry 277 above.

279 1782 October 11, Charleston
LOSENBERRY, Stephan, from New York state, shoemaker
New York Volunteers
Pass to South Carolina

280 1782 October 11, Charleston
GLEESON, Thomas, from Ireland, farmer
New York Volunteers
Pass to South Carolina

281 1782 October 13, Charleston
LONGLARE?, Henry, from Germany, distiller
King's American Regiment
Pass to Philadelphia

282 1782 October 17, James Island
SPENCER, Robert, from England, plasterer
33rd British Regiment
Pass to Virginia

283 1782 October 17, James Island
BRADLEY, Thomas, from Ireland, weaver
33rd British Regiment
Pass to Virginia

284 1782 October 18, Charleston
WEAVER, Henry, from Germany, butcher
Regiment von Benning
Pass to Stono
Research Notes: (a) According to Hetrina, 1:8208, soldier WEBER, Henrich, born 1751-1752, from Marburg, deserted from company 4, Garrison Regiment von Huyn, later von Benning, in October 1782.
(b) For Marburg, see Entry 206 above.

285 1782 October 18, Charleston
NICHOLAS, Christopher, from Germany, farmer
Regiment von Benning
Pass to Stono
Research Notes: (a) According to Hetrina, 1:5468, soldier NICOLAUS, Christoph, born 1753-1754, from Muenchhausen, Hessen, deserted from company 4, Garrison Regiment von Huyn, later von Benning, in October 1782.
(b) For Muenchhausen, see Entry 236 above.

286 1782 October 20, [Lark] Galley
BROWN, Thomas, from New York, sailor
Lark, Galley
Pass to Philadelphia

287 1782 October 20, [Lark] Galley
GULLION?, Frederick, from Ireland, sailor
Lark, Galley
Pass to Philadelphia

288 1782 October 23, Quarterhouse
MULHALON, --?, from Ireland, farmer
3rd British Regiment
Pass to South? Carolina
Research Note: There was a William MULHOLAND, from the Third British Regiment, who was a prisoner of war in 1778. See Clifford Neal Smith, British and German Deserters, Dischargees, and Prisoners of War Who May Have Remained in Canada and the United States, 1774-1783. British-American Genealogical Research Monograph Number 9, Part 2 (McNeal, AZ: Westland Publications, 1989), p. 13.

289 1782 October 23, Quarterhouse
DOWNEY, --?, from Ireland, farmer
3rd British Regiment
Pass to South? Carolina
Research Note: This soldier not mentioned in <u>Ibid</u>.

290 1782 October 23, Charleston
PULSOVER, Archibald, from Massachusetts, farmer
New York Volunteers
Pass to Boston

291 1782 October 23, Charleston
BOSS, John, from New York, farmer
New York Volunteers
Pass to Albany

292 1782 October 25, Charleston
SNYDER, John, from Germany, weaver
Regiment von Ditfurth
Pass to Pennsylvania
Research Notes: (a) According to <u>Hetrina</u>, 2:9630, soldier SCHNEIDER, Johannes, born 1750-1751, from Wehrshausen, Hessen, deserted from company 1, Regiment von Ditfurth, in September 1782.
(b) According to the Prussian census of 1871:
   (i) Hessen-Nassau, Regierungsbezirk Kassel, Kreis Marburg, Landgemeinde Wehrshausen. Total population 212 (201 Protestant, 10 Catholic).
   (ii) Hessen-Nassau, Regierungsbezirk Kassel, Kreis Hersfeld, Landgemeinde Wehrshausen. Total population 192 (all Protestant).
(c) Geographic coordinates: 50-48N 8-43E <u>and</u> 50-48N 9-53E, both in Hessen.
(d) According to <u>Preliminary Survey</u>, the Family History Center, Salt Lake City, has Wehrhausen* Justizamt [local court] records, 1831-1881.
*So spelled.

293 1782 October 25, Charleston
KEAN?, Conrad, from Germany, farmer
Regiment von Ditfurth
Pass to Pennsylvania
Research Notes: (a) According to <u>Hetrina</u>, 2:2565, soldier KUEHN, Konrad, born 1756-1757, from Cappel, Hessen, deserted from company 1, Regiment von Ditfurth, in September 1782.
(b) There are six villages of this name in West Germany, two in Hessen. According to the Prussian census of 1871:
   (i) Hessen-Nassau, Regierungsbezirk Kassel, Kreis Fritzlar, Landgemeinde Cappel (<u>or</u> Kappel). Total population 162 (152 Protestants, 7 Jews).
   (ii) Hessen-Nassau, Regierungsbezirk Kassel, Kreis Marburg, Landgemeinde Cappel. Total population 764 (753 Protestants).
(c) According to the <u>Preliminary Survey</u>, the Family History Center, Salt Lake City, has Cappel/Marburg local court and Standesamt [civil registry] records, 1808-1812.

294 1782 October 23, James Island
SPRINGER, John, from Germany, farmer
Regiment von Benning
Pass to Stono
Research Notes: (a) According to <u>Hetrina</u>, 1;7471, soldier SPRENGER, Johannes, Jg. [the younger], born 1755-1757, from Lischeid, Hessen, deserted from company 2, Garrison Regiment von Huyn, later von Benning, in October 1782.
(b) According to the Prussian census of 1871: Hessen-Nassau, Regierungsbezirk Kassel, Kreis Ziegenhain, Landgemeinde Lischeid. Total population 312 (all Protestant).
(c) Geographic coordinates: 50-55N 9-01E, Hessen.
(d) According to <u>Preliminary Survey</u>, the Family History Center, Salt Lake City, has Lischeid Obergericht [superior court] records, 1816-1846.

295 1782 October 23, James Island
WYMER, Barth., from Germany, shoemaker
Regiment von Benning
Pass to Stono
Research Notes: (a) According to <u>Hetrina</u>, 1:8276, soldier WEIMAR, Bartholomaeus, born 1754-1755, from Neukirchen, Hessen, deserted from company 1, Garrison Regiment von Huy, later von Benning, in October 1782.
(b) There are 27 villages of this name in West Germany, four in Hessen.
(c) According to the <u>Preliminary Survey</u>, the Family History Center, Salt Lake City, has Neukirchen/Huenfeld Standesamt records, 1874-1875; Neukirchen/Ziegenhain Standesamt [civil registry] and Justizamt [local court] records, 1768-1875.

296 1782 October 26, Charleston
McCOY, John, from Scotland, tailor
63rd British Regiment
Pass to Virginia

297 1782 October 26, Charleston
BRANHAM?/BRANT?, William, from Scotland, sailor
King's American Regiment
Pass to New England

298 1782 October 26, Charleston
CUMPTON, Abraham, from New York, farmer
New York Volunteers
Pass to New York state

299 1782 October 26, Charleston
READ, Georg, from Long Island, weaver
New York Volunteers
Pass to New York state

300 1782 October 26, Charleston
HALLOWELL, James, from Scotland, farmer
New York Volunteers
Pass to Camden

301 1682 October 26, Charleston
SHANNON, Nicholas?, from Ireland, smith
New York Volunteers
Pass to Philadelphia

302 1782 October 26, Charleston
MOTTS?, Jacob, from New York state, farmer
New York Volunteers
Pass to New York state

303 1782 October 26, Charleston
   EVERY, Isaac?, from New York state, spinning weaver
   New York Volunteers
   Pass to New York state

304 1782 October 30, Charleston
   KNOUF, Conrad, Sergeant, from Germany, shoemaker
   Regiment von Ditfurth
   Pass to Camden
   Research Notes: (a) According to Hetrina, 2:2078, corporal KNAUFF, Konrad, born 1747-1748, from Marburg, Hessen, deserted company 4, Regiment von Ditfurth, in September 1782.
   (b) For Marburg, see Entry 206 above.

305 1782 October 30, Charleston
   LEAT, John, from Germany, weaver
   Regiment von Ditfurth
   Pass to Camden
   Research Notes: (a) According to Hetrina, 2:6246, soldier LICH, Johannes, born 1755-1757, from Sterzhausen, Hessen, deserted company 4, Regiment von Ditfurth, first in August 1779 and again in September 1782.
   (b) According to the Prussian census of 1871, Hessen-Nassau, Regierungsbezirk Kassel, Kreis Marburg, Landgemeinde Sterzhausen. Total population 555 (almost all Protestant).
   (c) Geographic coordinates: 50-51N 8-42E, Hessen.
   (d) According to Preliminary Survey, the Family History Center, Salt Lake City, has Sterzhausen Standesamt [civil registry] records, 1808-1871.

306 1782 October, 30, Charles
   LONG, Ludwick, from Germany, farmer
   Regiment von Ditfurth
   Pass to Camden
   Research Notes: (a) According to Hetrina, 2:6088, soldier LANGE, Ludwig, born 1753-1756, from Somplar, Hessen, deserted from company 4, Regiment von Ditfurth, in September 1783! [This date may be a misprint in Hetrina.]
   (b) For Somplar, see Entry 235 above.

307 1782 October 30, Charleston
   SHEARER, Bind.?, from Germany, bricklayer
   Regiment von Ditfurth
   Pass to Camden
   Research Notes: (a) According to Hetrina, 2:9209, soldier SCHERRER, Balthasar, born 1758-1759, from Halgehausen, deserted company 5, Regiment von Ditfurth, in September 1782.
   (b) Also called Halgenhausen. According to the Prussian census of 1871, Hessen-Nassau, Regierungsbezirk Kassel, Kreis Frankfenberg, Landgemeinde Halgehausen. Total population 239 (all Protestant).
   (c) Geographic coordinates: 51-01N 8-56E, Hessen.

308 1782 October 30, Charleston
   WILSON, John, from Germany, flax? weaver
   Regiment von Angelelli
   Pass to Virginia
   Research Note: According to Hetrina, 1:8558, soldier WILSON, Jonas, from Isle of Wight, Virginia, served from 1779-1780 in company 3, Regiment von Lengerke; reported to have been granted land in 1780. [Identification very doubtful, but it might be that this man then joined Regiment von Angelelli for the southern campaign.]

309 1782 October 30, Charleston
   HOTER, George, from Germany, weaver
   Regiment von Angelelli
   Pass to Virginia
   Research Notes: (a) According to Hetrina, 3:8286, soldier HUETER, Georg, born 1745-1747, from Eschwege, Hessen, deserted from company 2, Regiment Erbprinz [Crown Prince], in September 1782. He reenlisted in his unit in June 1783. [Most men and officers from Regiment Erbprinz were captured at Yorktown and imprisoned in Frederickstown, Maryland; the unit was apparently not in the campaign in the Carolinas. It may have been that this man was detached from his troop unit to serve with Regiment von Angelelli. However, identification must be considered doubtful.]
   (b) According to the Prussian census of 1871, Hessen-Nassau, Regierungsbezirk Kassel, Kreis Eschwege, Stadtgemeinde Eschwege. Total population 7371 (6764 Protestants, 89 Catholics, 509 Jews).
   (c) Geographic coordinates: 51-11N 10-04E Hessen.
   (d) According to Preliminary Survey, the Family History Center, Salt Lake City, has Eschwege communal records, Standesamt [civil registry], and Justizamt [local court] files, 1790-1874.

310 1782 October 30, Charleston
   MITCHELL, Thomas, from England, sailor
   Brown's [Corps]
   Pass to Georgetown

311 1782 October 30, Charleston
   COOK, Samuel, from England, farmer
   New York Volunteers
   Pass to New York state

312 1782 October 30, Charleston
   LAWRENCE, Richard, from New York state, farmer
   New York Volunteers
   Pass to New York state

313 1782 November 01, Charleston
   LIMBERT, William, from Germany, cooper
   Regiment von Knoblauch
   Pass to Camden
   Research notes: (a) According to Hetrina, 3:8989, soldier LIMPERT, Wilhelm, born 1759-1760, from Kassel, Hessen, was recruited into company 1, Regiment von Wissenbach, later von Knoblauch, in March 1780. [This man appears only on one muster roll and may have been overlooked in later rolls.]
   (b) According to Preliminary Survey, the Family History Center, Salt Lake City, has voluminous records from Kassel, including Evangelical church records 1755-1812 and 1866-1940; Standesamt [civil registry] and court records at several levels; there is also a military church [chaplaincy] record.

314 1782 November 01, Charleston
    NOWMAN, John, from Germany, farmer
    Regiment von Ditfurth
    Pass to Camden
    Research Notes: (a) According to Hetrina, 2:7399 and 2:7400, there were two soldiers of this name:
      (i) NAUMANN, Johannes, born 1748-1749, from Oberweimar, Hessen, who deserted from company 5, Regiment von Ditfurth, in September 1782.
      (ii) NAUMANN, Johannes, born 1755-1756, from Sterzhausen, Hessen, who deserted from company 4, Regiment von Ditfurth, in September 1782.
    (b) According to the Prussian census of 1871, there are four villages named Weimar in Hessen:
      (i) Hessen-Nassau, Regierungsbezirk Kassel, Landkreis Kassel, Landgemeinde Weimar. Total population 931 (all Protestant).
      (ii) Hessen-Nassau, Regierungsbezirk Kassel, Kreis Marburg, Landgemeinde Niederweimar. Total populatin 408 (all Protestant).
      (iii) Hessen-Nassau, Regierungsbezirk Kassel, Kreis Marburg, Landgemeinde Oberweimar. Total population 278 (all Protestant). [This is the most likely place of origin for this soldier.]
      (iv) Hessen-Nassau, Regierungsbezirk Kassel, Kreis Marburg, Landgemeinde Cyriaxweimar. Total population 129 (all Protestant).
    For Sterzhausen, see Entry 305 above.
    (c) Geographic coordinates for Oberweimar: 50-45N 8-42E, Hessen.
    (d) According to Preliminary Survey, the Family History Center, Salt Lake City, has Oberwiemar* Justizamt [local court] records, 1808-1882.
    *So spelled.

315 1782 November 02, Charleston
    JONES, Gilese, from Wales, farmer
    19th British Regiment
    Pass to Hillsboro

316 1782 October 31, Charleston
    BORNE, John, from Germany, farmer
    Regiment von Ditfurth
    Pass to Camden
    Research Note: (a) According to Hetrina, 2:1198, soldier BORN, Paul, born 1753-1754, fron Elnhausen, Hessen, deserted from company 1, Regiment von Ditfurth in September 1782. [Identification uncertain]
    (b) According to the Prussian census of 1871, Hessen-Nassau, Regierungsbezirk Kassel, Kreis Marburg, Landgemeinde Ellnhausen*. Total population 462 (455 Protestants). *So spelled.
    (c) Geographic coordinates: 50-48N 8-41E, Hessen.
    (d) According to the Preliminary Survey, the Family History Center, Salt Lake City, has Elnhausen Standesamt [civil registry] records, 1808-1812.

317 1782 November 09, Charleston
    McDERMOTT, Angus, from Scotland, farmer
    Delinson's? [De Lancy's] [Corps]
    Pass to North Carolina

318 1782 November 09, Charleston
    NILE?, Benjamin, from Rhode Island, farmer
    Greyhound [ship?]
    Pass to Georgetown

319 1782 November 09, Charleston
    KELLY, Abner, from Massachusetts, farmer
    Greyhound [ship?]
    Pass to Georgetown

320 1782 November 09, Charleston
    ROBINS, Enoch, from Massachusetts, farmer
    Greyhound [ship?]
    Pass to Georgetown

321 1782 November 09, Charleston
    IRVINE, William, from South Carolina, farmer
    Greyhound [ship?]
    Pass to South Carolina

322 1782 November 12, [place not given]
    HARRIS, Thomas, American, farmer
    Duke of Cumberland? [Regiment]
    Pass to Virginia

323 1782 November 11, Charleston
    GRIFFITH, Zachariah, American?, farmer
    Duke of Cumberland? [Regiment]
    Pass to Maryland

324 1782 November 15, [place not given]
    ADAMS, Thomas, from St. Cruise?*, sailor
    Bellisarico [ship?]
    Pass to Pennsylvania
    *Probably St. Croix, West Indies.

325 1782 November 18, [place not given]
    HOPKINS, Toney, American, [craft not given]
    Bellisarico [ship?]
    Pass to Rhode Island

326 1782 December 02, [place not given]
    STEEL?, John, from England, farmer
    [illegible]
    Pass to Cambden [Camden]

327 1782 December 02, [place not given]
    WOOD, James, from England, weaver
    33rd British Regiment
    Pass to Cambden [Camden]

328 1782 December 02, [place not given]
    HOLMES, William, from Ireland, tailor
    33rd British Regiment
    Pass to Cambden [Camden]

329 1782 December 02, [place not given]
    WILKINSON?, William, from England, cabinetmaker
    33rd British Regiment
    Pass to Cambden [Camden]

330 1782 December 03, [place not given]
    CAMBELL [CAMPBELL], Duncan, from Ireland, sailor
    [illegible], galley
    Pass to Philadelphia? or Georgetown?

331 1782 December 11, James Island
   LINK?, Zachariah, from Germany, [craft not given]
   60th British Regiment
   Pass to Dutch Fork?

332 [No data herein, but see Entry 504.]

333 1782 December 11, James Island
   KNORY?, Christian?/Henry?, from Germany, shoemaker
   60th British Regiment
   Pass to Dutch Fork?

334 1782 December 11, James Island
   PARIS, Baptist, from France, blacksmith
   60th British Regiment
   Pass to country [unspecified destination?]

335 1782 December 11, James Island
   TRUIT, James, American, farmer
   S.* Loyalists
   Pass to North Carolina
   *South Carolina?

336 1782 December 13, James Island
   JOHNSTON, William, from England, sailor
   S.* Loyalists
   Pass to South Carolina
   *South Carolina?

337 1782 December 13, [place not given]
   WOLF, Morte, from Germany, farmer
   60th British Regiment
   Pass to country [unspecified destination?]

338 1782 December 14, [place not given]
   HARMAR, Samuel, from England, shoemaker
   22nd British Regiment
   Pass to country [unspecified destination?]

339 1782 December 15, [place not given]
   MAP?/MASS?, John, from England, [craft not given]
   60th British Regiment
   Pass to North Carolina

340 1782 December 15, [place not given]
   SMITH, Daniel, from Germany, [craft not given]
   60th British Regiment
   Pass to South? Carolina

341 1782 December 15, [place not given]
   REED, John, from England, [craft not given]
   60th British Regiment
   Pass to Pennsylvania

342 1782 December 15, [place not given]
   ESELMIRE?/EFELMIRE?, John, from Germany, carpenter
   60th British Regiment
   Pass to Pennsylvania

343 1782 December 15, [place not given]
   AGLINTON?, William, from England, nailer
   60th British Regiment
   Pass to Charleston

344 1782 December 15, [place not given]
   CELLINGTON?, Thomas, from England, blacksmith
   60th British Regiment
   Pass to Charleston

345 1782 December 15, [place not given]
   MADDIN, Daniel, from Ireland, weaver
   60th British Regiment
   Pass to North Carolina

346 1782 December 15, [place not given]
   SCOTT?, Daniel, from England, [craft not given]
   60th British Regiment
   Pass to country [unspecified destination?]

347 1782 December 15, [place not given]
   JONES, Henry, from Ireland, weaver
   64th British Regiment
   Pass to country [unspecified destination?]

348 1782 December 16, [place not given]
   McFAUL, John, from Ireland, [craft not given]
   60th British Regiment
   Pass to country [unspecified destination?]

349 1782 December 16, [place not given]
   NASH, Morris, from Ireland, [craft not given]
   60th British Regiment
   Pass to country [unspecified location?]

350 1782 December 16, [place not given]
   STEWART, John, from Scotland, weaver
   71st British Regiment
   Pass to North Carolina

351 1782 December 16, [place not given]
   RUCHBARK, William, from Germany, farmer
   60th British Regiment
   Pass to North Carolina

352 1782 December 16, [place not given]
   OSBURN, Titus, from England, button maker
   60th British Regiment
   Pass to Pennsylvania

353 1782 December 16, [place not given]
   KRICH?, Frederick, from Germany, farmer
   60th British Regiment
   Pass to Virginia

354 1782 December 16, [place not given]
   WOLCOT?, William, from Scotland, [craft not given]
   [Military unit not given]
   Pass to Virginia

355 1782 December 16, [place not given]
    BURK, Patrick, from Ireland, [craft not given]
    [Military unit not given]
    Pass to Virginia

356 1782 December 16, [place not given]
    PAPANIN, Lewis, from Hesse, carpenter
    [Military unit not given]
    [Pass destination not given]

501 1781 [1782?] December 14, [place not given]
    BANTHAM? John, [no further description]
    1st Maryland Regiment
    Pass to go hunting
    [Entry 501 in front papers to register.]

502 1781 [1782?] December 14, [place not given]
    WEAVER, Benjamin [no further description]
    1st North Carolina Regiment
    Pass to go hunting
    [Entry 502 in front papers to register.]

503 1781 [1782?] December 14, [place not given]
    AMBROSE, John, [no further description]
    2nd North Carolina Regiment
    Pass to go hunting
    [Entry 503 in front papers to register.]

504 1782? December --?, [no place given]
    MILLER, Isaiah, from England, farmer
    17th British Regiment
    Pass to Connecticut?
    [This is probably the missing Entry 332, as the notation is on the facing page at Entry 316 of the register.]

SURNAME INDEX

(By Entry Number)

ACHKINS, 012
ACHKINS. See also ATKINS
ACTIAN, 127
ADAMS, 324
ADLER, 036
AGLINTON, 343
ALEXANDER, 223
ALLANTHORPE, 254
AMBROSE, 503
AMICK, 224
ARTIS, 222
ATKINS, 094
ATKINS. See also ACHKINS
BAKER, 146
BANTHAM, 501
BARNUM, 057
BARUCH, 166
BATES, 160
BAUCH, 166
BAUCKER, 166
BECKER, 146
BENDER, 024
BENNET, 233
BERD, 217
BORN, 316
BORNE, 316
BORNMANN, 278
BOSS, 291
BRADLEY, 095, 283
BRAKE, 051
BRANHAM, 297
BRANT, 297
BRENNEWALT, 033
BRENWALT, 033
BROWN, 071, 250, 286
BRUNAMAN, 278
BRUNCK, 051
BURK, 355
BURRELL, 005
CALDWELL, 168
CALLEY, 167
CAMBELL, 330
CAMPBELL, 330
CANNON. See GANNON
CARLE, 208
CARLESTON, 181
CARLOH, 135
CARMAN, 249
CARSKADON, 134
CARSON, 155
CASPER. See GASPER
CASSAT. See GASSAT
CASSELMANN, 121
CATON, 022
CELLINGTON, 344
CHARLES, 208
CLARK, 189
CLEMENS, 086
CLEMENZ, 086
CLEPROD, 102
CLINE, 014
CO---?, 132
COHOON, 090
COMPTON. See CUMPTON
CONNELL, 219
CONNER, 050
CONWAY, 164, 165
COOK, 311
CORNELL, 219
COTTON, 046
CRAWFORD, 070, 267
CREUTZBERG, 214
CRITZBURGH, 214
CROFORD, 267
CROMER, 264
CROSS, 087
CROUS, 013
CUMPTON, 298
DAILY, 178
DAWSONS, 118
DEFERT, 192
DEFOOTE, 193
DEFOOTE. See also FOOT
DENNIS, 019
DICKES, 069
DITTSCHAR, 069
DIXON, 179
DOBBS, 049
DOER, 153
DONALD, 174

DOWNEY, 289
DOWNING, 136
DUNIGAN, 138
EDLER, 036
EFELMIRE, 342
ELLIOTT, 112
ELLISON, 109
ELLMORE, 088
ELLSWORTH, 111
ENNIS, 018
ESELMAN, 185
ESELMIRE, 342
EUTUS, 018
EVERY, 303
FAIRES, 089
FANNING, 157
FINNIS, 019
FISCHER, 207, 238
FLAGLER, 158
FOOT, 243
FOOT. See also DEFOOTE
FRIESLAND, 048
FRISELAND, 048
FULLERTON, 114
GAFNEY, 059
GANNON, 062
GASPEE, 020
GASPER, 020
GASSAT, 196
GAYIMAN, 007
GEORGE, 248
GIMBEL, 277
GITSINGER, 227
GLEESON, 280
GLEIN, 014
GLENN, 170
GOODWIN, 075

GORDON, 107
GOSLING, 242
GRAUSS, 013
GREGORY, 073
GRIFFITH, 323
GRIFFY, 074
GULLION, 287
GUTMUTH, 194
HALLOWELL, 300
HANDKAMMER, 148
HARMAR, 338
HARRIS, 037, 065, 322
HART, 104
HASE, 065
HAWKINS, 188
HAYNES, 163
HEATH, 251, 252
HEIDER, 137
HEIDERMANN, 141
HEINEMANN, 141
HENEISEN, 032
HERT, 104
HERTER, 031
HESSE, 065
HETSWORTH, 010
HIGGS, 272
HOFMASTER, 235
HOFMEISTER, 235
HOLMES, 177, 328
HOPKINS, 325
HORTER, 031
HOSCH, 065
HOSERMAN, 121
HOTER, 309
HUETER, 309
IRVINE, 321
JACKSON, 175, 218, 258, 271

JACOB, 246
JAKOB, 246
JOHNSTON, 336
JOHNSTONE, 221
JONES, 076, 125, 315, 347
JUNGERMANN, 066
KANAKA, 067
KASPAR. See GASPER
KEAN, 293
KEEMAN, 144
KELLY, 319
KENNEDY, 115
KENT, 043, 253
KESSLER, 142, 145
KESTLER, 142, 145
KIMBALL, 277
KING, 039
KING. See also KOENIG
KLAPROT, 102
KLEIN, 014
KNAUFF, 304
KNORY, 333
KNOUF, 304
KOENIG, 067
KOSERMAN, 121
KRAUSS, 013
KRICH, 353
KUEHN, 293
LAMBERT, 041
LAMBERT. See also LIMBERT, LIMPERT
LAND, 265
LANGE, 306
LANMAN, 240
LAPS, 275
LASLIE, 097
LAWRENCE, 312
LEAT, 305

LEATE, 159
LEIBRA, 180
LEIDOFF, 128
LEISGE, 207
LENDON, 011
LESLIE. See LASLIE
LEYDORF, 128
LICH, 305
LIDSTER, 053
LIMBERT, 313
LIMPERT, 313
LIMBERT, LIMPERT. See also LAMBERT
LINCKER, 245
LINCOLN, 083
LINK, 331
LINKER, 245
LINSLEY, 023
LISHER, 207
LODEN, 092
LONG, 201, 306
LONGLARE, 281
LOSENBERRY, 279
MADDIN, 345
MANURE, 008
MAP, 339
MARIOT, 009
MARLO, 030
MARSHALL, 110
MASS, 339
MATHEWS, 234
MAZICK, 195
McALLISTER, 103
McCARTY, 123
McCLAINE, 055
McCLOUSS, 029
McCOY, 045, 211, 296
McCRAE, 003

McCREA, 184
McCULLOP, 269
McDERMOTT, 317
McDONALD, 001, 063, 171, 172, 173, 174, 210
McDONNOUGH, 100
McDOUGAL, 151
McELROY, 241
McFAUL, 348
McKAY, 257
McKENNA, 072
McKENZIE, 256
McLANE, 244
McLAUGHLIN, 247, 270
McMAHON, 047
McMULLEN, 079
McMULLIN, 232
McQUIN, 004
MERLO, 030
MERLS, 030
MEYER, 035, 213
MILLER, 025, 154
MILLINGTON, 103
MITCHELL, 081, 310
MITZNER, 150
MONRO, 216
MORGAN, 239
MOSER, 147
MOSES, 199
MOTT, 162,
MOTTS, 302
MUELLER, 025
MUETZE, 150
MULHALON, 288
MULHOLAND, 288
MULLEN, 098
MURPHEY, 054
MURRAY, 122, 149

MURRY, 122
MYER, 035
MYERS, 213
NASH, 349
NAUMANN, 314
NICHOLAS, 285
NICOLAUS, 285
NILE, 318
NIXON, 197
NORRIS, 228
NOWMAN, 314
OSBURN, 352
OWENS, 021
PAINE, 026
PAPANIN, 356
PARIS, 105, 334
PARKER, 082
PATTERSON, 002, 268
PEREZ, 105
PFINGST, 068
PINKS, 068
PITTS, 117, 126
PO---?, 084
PORTER, 099, 140
POTTS, 126
POWELL, 056
PULSOVER, 290
READ, 299
REED, 341
REEMAN, 144
REITH, 206
REZAR, 230, 231
RIEMANN, 144
RINGLEB, 129
RINGLEBEN, 129
ROBERTSON, 183
ROBINS, 320

ROBINSON, 113
ROCK, 133
ROYER, 230, 231
RUCHBARK, 351
RYAL, 120
RYAN, 230, 231
SAINTT, 130
SAMPSON, 027
SANMAN, 240
SARLOH, 135
SCHAEFFER, 034
SCHATZ, 237
SCHELLHASE, 052
SCHERRER, 307
SCHMIDT, 015
SCHMIDT. See also SMITH
SCHNEIDER, 292
SCOFIELD, 096, 204
SCOTT, 091, 346
SEELY, 044
SEIBRI, 180
SEITZLER, 226
SENDON, 011
SHAFFER, 034
SHANNON, 116, 301
SHEARER, 307
SHELHURST, 052
SIMMONS, 205
SIMS, 261
SISCHER, 207
SKEPELER, 085
SMETHERS, 273
SMITH, 015, 040, 106, 340
SMITHERS, 273
SNYDER, 292
SODEN, 092
SOLDAN, 236

SOLTER, 236
SOUTHERLAND, 078
SPENCER, 006, 282
SPOTZ, 237
SPRENGER, 294
SPRINGER, 294
STAFFERS, 042
STAR, 080
STAUB, 200
STEEL, 326
STEIMBY, 198
STEPHAN, 042
STERNS, 202
STEVENSON, 191
STEWARD, 028
STEWART, 350
STILL, 038
STONE, 058
STOREF, 200
STOUF, 200
STUART, 209
SULTHAN, 236
SUTTES, 225
TAYLOR, 203
TEATE, 159
TEED, 108
THOMPSON, 187
THORER, 153
THORNE, 093
TINNIS, 019
TREWIT, 255
TRUIT, 335
TYLER, 119
ULM, 182
VAUGHAN, 212
VEITCH, 229
VERNER, 176

VERNON, 176

VISCHELL, 101

WABERTON, 139

WADSWORTH, 215

WAITE, 161

WALPER, 017

WALPOLEN, 017

WALPOLER, 017

WALTER, 274

WALTERS, 262

WALTON, 262

WATKINS, 259, 260

WEAVER, 284, 502

WEBER, 284

WEIMAR, 295

WELKINSON, 077

WELKINSON. See also WILKINSON

WERNER, 016

WERSEN, 016

WETZEL, 101

WHEELER, 263

WHITE, 060, 064

WHITLOCK, 156

WHITMAN, 186

WILKINSON, 329

WILKINSON. See also WELKINSON

WILLIAMS, 124

WILSON, 190, 308

WINTERBOTTOM, 276

WITT, 152

WITZEL, 101

WOLCOT, 354

WOLF, 337

WOLLENHAUPT, 275

WOOD, 327

WOODWARD, 220

WORKSMAN, 169

WRIGHT, 206

WYMER, 295

YEO, 131

YOUNGMAN, 066

ZIMMER, 143

--?, 266, 332

--? (3 officers and 27 privates not named) 061

www.ingramcontent.com/pod-product-compliance
Lightning Source LLC
Chambersburg PA
CBHW080922180426
43192CB00040B/2663